THINGS THAT BREAK

I0139620

Sherry Kramer

BROADWAY PLAY PUBLISHING INC
New York
www.broadwayplaypub.com
info@broadwayplaypub.com

Cover photo by Tony Cisek

Originally publised by B P P I in *Plays By Sherry Kramer*
in December 2000
First printing, this edition: March 2019
I S B N: 978-0-88145-802-2

Book design: Marie Donovan
Page make-up: Adobe InDesign
Typeface: Palatino

THINGS THAT BREAK premiered at Theater of the
First Amendment (Rick Davis, Artistic Director; Kevin
Murray, Managing Director). It opened on 19 March
1997 with the following cast and creative contributors:

NURSE PITKIN	Rosemary Knower
JACKIE	Jennifer Mendenhall
ELIZABETH	Nancy Robinette
PETER	Kyle Pruitt
VICTOR	Ralph Cosham
DOCTOR GLASS/MACKIE	Irv Ziff
STELLA	Barbara Rappaport
Ensemble	Adam Graham, Aimee Gabrielle Koller,
	Brent Morris, Gregory Rosenberg,
	Michael Thomas, Carly Van Orman

Director	Bill Foeller
Set designer	Tony Cisek
Lighting designer	Martha Mountain
Costume designer	Howard Vincent Kurtz
Sound designer	David Maddox
Dramaturge	Kristin Johnson Nastashi

THINGS THAT BREAK was written with the help
and support of The New Dramatists, Jessie Allen, The
MacDowell Colony, The Dorset Colony, and The Albee
Foundation. Special thanks to Rick Davis and Kevin
Murray.

In memory of Bill Foeller

To have Bill's calm and wonderful spirit guiding us was a special joy. He never wavered from his vision of the play. His work from start to finish was magnificent, and he did it without compromising, arguing, demanding, or complaining. He would simply ask for what was possible, and accept that we would give him our best work.

Bill made us all better than we had been, better than we had dared to be, and he did it quietly, by force of ideas and commitment, by vision and imagination, by an accumulated wisdom that never had to proclaim itself but was revealed in action and by degrees.

His creative gifts seemed as inexhaustible as he did. It is our great sorrow that we will not have the chance to work with him again.

The cast, creative and artistic staff Theater of the First Amendment production of THINGS THAT BREAK

CHARACTERS

JACKIE DEMERY, *in her late twenties. She is a glass maker. She dresses artistically.*

PETER DEMERY, *her twin. He's an investment banker. He's wearing an expensive suit with the tie loosened, and the shirt a bit too wrinkled.*

ELIZABETH DEMERY, *their mother. She is in her late forties. She is still a beautiful woman, and there is a great sweetness to her face. She is wearing a shirtwaist dress in a jewel tone, the kind of dress women in cities wear.*

NURSE PITKIN, *Head Story Nurse. One of those ageless looking angels of mercy. She carries a Lucite clipboard, with charts clipped to it. She wears one of those retractable pens that is pinned to her blouse. And her uniform is dazzling white. Pristine, starched, one hundred percent cotton—it looks slightly archaic, perhaps from the forties in some way. But not too out of style. She is also wearing one of those classic nurse caps. There is a little border of blood red around the rim of the cap. She is wearing the perfect amount of makeup, white hose, and white pumps—no sensible nurse's clodhoppers for her.*

VICTOR DEMERY, *the twins' father, ELIZABETH's husband. He is tall, and strong, and gentle, and under anesthesia.*

Doubled characters:

JOSEPHINE *and* STELLA, *professional old ladies, played by different actors each time, male and female*

DR GLASS *and* THE OPERATING TEAM, *four doctors, mostly males, can sing*

SINGING TELEGRAM, *youngish, male or female, can tap dance and sing*

CANDY STRIPER, *youngish, can tap dance and sing*

The play is written to be performed with a minimum cast of ten. In the original production, STELLA *was always played by the same actress, and two additional ensemble members were cast.*

SETTING

PART ONE

The waiting room of an old, big hospital. Along the upstage wall, a vending machine. The seating area down stage—a couch, a coffee table, a couple of comfortable chairs.

To one side, the restroom area. Two stalls.

Opposite side—a revolving door that leads into the operating theater, which is not visible.

There are also tall upstage swinging doors, leading into an area of great heat and light.

The waiting room area is extremely shallow.

PART TWO

The waiting room has been miniaturized, so that it is approximately one-third its previous size.

The rest of the stage is now the operating theater—but one which incorporates state of the art elements of an operating theater with anachronistic ones, so that some tools are antique, museum pieces, etc. And some aspects of the room do not directly suggest an operating room at all, but refer to other places, where men and women work with their hands.

The essence of being human is that one does not seek perfection, that one is sometimes willing to commit sins for the sake of loyalty, and that one is prepared in the end to be defeated and broken up by life, which is the inevitable price of fastening one's love upon other human individuals.
George Orwell

All true stories end in death.
Ernest Hemingway

PROLOGUE

(The three actresses playing JACKIE, ELIZABETH, *and* NURSE PITKIN *appear, in front of the curtain. They are all wearing identical black velvet evening gowns, beautifully made, gorgeous to look at.)*

(The actress playing NURSE PITKIN *is holding a beautiful, hand-blown champagne glass. It is so thin, so fine, that it almost appears to float in her hand. It is a traditional champagne shape, with perhaps some threads or twists in the stem, but no color—it is clear, brilliant glass. There is champagne in the glass. She holds the glass up in her hand, as if at the beginning of a toast, and surveys the audience.)*

NURSE PITKIN: This...is not the first word of this play. *(She places the champagne glass on the floor, near the edge of the stage, out of her way.)*

JACKIE: The first word of this play is glass.

(A large sheet of glass is handed to her from the wings/floats down from the flies/emerges from the floor, whatever. The sheet is probably three feet high, three feet wide—however large safety requirements require it to be. She steadies the glass.)

NURSE PITKIN: But not that glass, or this glass.

(They reach into cleverly concealed pockets in their gowns. The gowns function as wondrously designed overalls— they are stuffed with tools, braces, hinges, everything they need to secure the sheets of glass to create a self-supporting

shield. They continue to work on the shield throughout this prologue.)

ELIZABETH: This glass is safety glass. This glass—

NURSE PITKIN: —and this glass is again not the first word of this play—

ELIZABETH: —this glass has been subjected to rigorous tests. Calibrations made to many decimal points have been duly noted, and written down, on official pieces of paper.

JACKIE: Documents have been signed, stating that this piece of glass—

(Another piece of glass appears, in the same manner as before—or perhaps, a more stunning or less stunning way.)

JACKIE: —and this piece of glass—are all absolutely safe.

NURSE PITKIN: We are assuring you of the safety of these pieces of glass because it is important that you are assured. This is the theater. Should danger, or the illusion of danger occur at the theater, it is important that it stay on its side of an illusory line, right here— *(She touches the edge of the stage with her toe.)* Danger— here. Safety—there. This is the theater, and in the theater, your safety comes first.

JACKIE: It is illegal to yell fire in a crowded theater. Fortunately, the first word of this play is not fire.

NURSE PITKIN: If the first word of this play were fire, and if the first thing you were going to see were fire, and not glass, then the fire marshal, with rigorous tests and official documents not unlike the ones that I have assured you have been rigorously conducted and officially signed concerning glass, would have certified the fire as absolutely safe.

JACKIE: It is not illegal to yell glass in a crowded theater.

ELIZABETH: In fact, if a tornado of sufficient speed and destruction were about to descend upon us, it would in all likelihood be considered a courtesy to yell glass, so that you could all double over in your seats and cover your eyes, except there is rarely any glass in a theater, crowded or otherwise.

JACKIE: Occasionally, in the chandeliers.

ELIZABETH: In the Broadway houses, at the bar, on the mezzanine.

NURSE PITKIN: But that, as a rule, is about it.

ELIZABETH: So there is rarely any reason for anyone in the theater to cover their eyes.

NURSE PITKIN: It would be a counterproductive thing to do at any time, and completely unnecessary tonight, because this glass—

(A third sheet of glass appears.)

NURSE PITKIN: —is here for your protection.

JACKIE: Like the paper strips on motel toilet seats when we were kids.

NURSE PITKIN: Wasn't it nice to know they cared, back then?

ELIZABETH: Don't you feel the loss of that protection, now that it has been replaced with a foil wrapped chocolate mint, positioned carefully near the pillow on the motel sheets?

NURSE PITKIN: I would have liked to put a little chocolate mint on each of your seats, tonight. I would have liked that, a lot. If the first word of this play were chocolate—well, it would be a different play.

ELIZABETH: I wish it were. It would be so much easier, to walk out on stage, knowing that each and everyone of you has got something dark—and sweet—and soft—melting in your mouth.

JACKIE: But you don't.

(The shield is completed, three sided, open on upstage side.)

NURSE PITKIN: The first word of this play is glass, and I couldn't put a little foil wrapped piece of broken glass on each of your seats tonight, even if I wanted to. *(She picks up the champagne glass, holds it up, toasting the audience. She is to one side of the barrier.)* To things—

ELIZABETH: To things—

JACKIE: To things that—

ELIZABETH: Break.

JACKIE: Break.

NURSE PITKIN: Break.

(NURSE PITKIN drains down the champagne in one grand gulp.)

(Blackout as she lets the glass fall, behind the barrier, so that the audience hears, but does not see it shatter just at the moment of darkness.)

END OF PROLOGUE

PART ONE

(Curtain up on the waiting room at Saint Mary's Hospital.
PETER DEMERY *is sitting on a chair, facing out. He is
bending over the small glass coffee table in front of him,
where a Scrabble board is in play. A folded up* Wall Street
Journal *beside him.* ELIZABETH DEMERY, *his mother,
is sitting on the sofa. On the floor beside her is an ample
knitting bag, filled to overflowing with yarn and half knitted
projects.)*

PETER: *(Putting his letter tiles down on the board.)* Glass.
G-L-A-S-S. *(He reaches for the scoring pad.)*

ELIZABETH: *(Looking up from her knitting, says directly
into the air in front of her.)* This is killing me. *(And
resumes knitting, calmly)*

PETER: Four for G. One for—

ELIZABETH: This is killing me.

PETER: Did you say something, Mom?

ELIZABETH: *(Looks up. Surprised that he thinks she has.)*
Me? No.

PETER: You're sure you didn't…I mean I…

ELIZABETH: I maybe cleared my throat. That's all.

PETER: *(Shrugs)* Okay. *(Back to Scrabble)* Four for G.

ELIZABETH: This is killing me. Except, of course, that
it might not be killing me. Everything might turn out
all right, in which case, this would not be killing me.

In which case, this would just be—making me strong.
After all, what doesn't kill you, makes you strong.

NURSE PITKIN: *(She flings open the door leading into the theater, from the back of the house, and sweeps down the aisle. Everything about her manner suggests that she is in absolute charge, and we will all be just fine.)* Hello. I'm Nurse Pitkin. And the first thing I'd like to say is that all our patients are special.

But all their stories are the same.

PETER: One for L.

NURSE PITKIN: *(She has ascended onto the stage.)* I can say this, because I'm the Head Story Nurse here at Saint Mary's.

PETER: One for A.

NURSE PITKIN: Saint Mary's. The hospital with the three Cs—Care, Concern, and Compassion—engraved in granite on the admitting room wall.

PETER: And two total for the S's.

NURSE PITKIN: I wasn't always a Story Nurse. For a long time, I was June Pitkin, Head Dialysis Nurse. It was a rewarding, fulfilling charge.

ELIZABETH: I think that *that's* what's killing me. Yes. That's it. What is killing me is not knowing whether this is killing me, or making me strong.

NURSE PITKIN: I had the hands for the work. But not the temperament for the job. Kidney problems were too local, too limiting for me. And when a kidney breaks down—well, just look at the way the word breaks down. Kidneys—K-I-D-N-E-Y-S.
Kid kids keys
den dens
din dines sin kin
kind kinds

send ends
ski skid sky ides side dies...
You'd be amazed at how many words have dying in
them. You really would. Almost as if the language had
a death wish, built right in.

ELIZABETH: After all, if it turns out that this is killing
me, rather than just making me strong, that's exactly
what I'll have to be. Because if everything I have ever
believed is true, I won't have any choice.
I'll have to be strong.

NURSE PITKIN: So I've put kidney work far behind me.
And who wouldn't, really, if given the chance? What's
dialysis all about, really...I'll tell you. You clean out
the machine, you hook up the patient, you clean out
the patient, you unhook the patient, you clean out the
machine. It's assembly line work.

PETER: That's eight all together. Triple word score.
Twenty-four.

NURSE PITKIN: It's still just nuts and bolts. It's still just
connect this to that. This to that. Thisness and thatness.

ELIZABETH: I think, now that I really think about it, that
that's what is killing me. Yes. What is really killing me
is— *(It just barely, precisely, eludes her.)* Damn. I can't tell
the difference! This *is* killing me, and I still have to sit
here and be strong! There's no difference! What doesn't
kill you makes you strong... Bullshit! *(She covers her
mouth with her hand, shocked at herself for even thinking
such a word.)* Bullshit. Bullshit. *(She's enjoying it.)* Bull...
shit. I never really thought the word bullshit before.
Damn and hell were as far as I had to go.

*(PETER throws down his Scrabble score pad, and goes toward
the Ladies' Restroom. NURSE PITKIN follows him.)*

NURSE PITKIN: *(Revealing the interior of the Ladies
Restroom in some ingenious way)* But, to make a long

story short—I got out of this and that. I traded all of that and this in, for the overall narrative. The scope, the scale, and the larger casts, that come with the duties of the Head Story Nurse.

PETER: *(Tapping on the restroom door)* Jackie? Jackie? It's your turn...Jackie?

(No response from JACKIE. PETER *sticks his head in through the door. Lights up on the Ladies Restroom. There are two stalls, or the suggestion of stalls, and women's legs are visible in each of them.* JACKIE *is standing in front of the mirror, playing with her hair. She has a brush in one hand, and a handful of clips and bobby pins in the other.)*

PETER: Jackie—NO! Jackie, not your hair!

*(*PETER *rushes into the bathroom but* JACKIE *ignores him, continues messing with her hair.)*

PETER: Jackie, your hair looks fine. JACKIE!!! JACKIE THERE IS NOTHING WRONG WITH YOUR HAIR!

JACKIE: *(Holding out her brush for him to hold)* Hold this.

PETER: No way.

JACKIE: Why not?

PETER: I won't be an enabler.

JACKIE: An enabler? Oh, my God. You're in therapy.

PETER: I am not. I'm in counseling. Couples counseling.

JACKIE: You think I don't know what kind of word enabler is?

NURSE PITKIN: *(Has entered the restroom as well, from a nonspecific entrance point. Her uniform has slightly transformed—she's hiked up her skirt, opened up her blouse, and is now pulling on a long white pair of opera length gloves.)* Enabler, by the way— *(She folds down a hidden panel in the wall, which becomes a shelf for a large white top hat. She takes the brush from* JACKIE, *with great flourish.)* —

is not a word. Officially. Oh, I have no doubt that it will make its way into the dictionaries eventually. That is the beauty of the lexicon of illness. You cannot cure an illness until you have a name for it. Naming a disease is the first and most important step in the search for the words that will cure it.

ELIZABETH: Bullshit. It feels good. Glad I saved it for an emergency.

(JACKIE *is still working at her hair.*)

PETER: Jackie—come on. Mom's sitting out there alone—

JACKIE: Then you go out and sit with her. I can't come. I can't come out until I get it right.

PETER: Stop it! Stop it NOW! Your hair looks fine. Stop trying to make it perfect. When it comes to hair there is no perfect. What would be the point of perfect? HAIR IS JUST HAIR!

(NURSE PITKIN *assists* JACKIE *in all her efforts with her hair, performing various magic act gestures with the pins, clips, et cetera, that* JACKIE *needs or hands to her.* NURSE PITKIN *pulls an astounding variety of hair accessories from the hat throughout the scene—curling irons, a blow dryer, falls, clips, and clamps and nets. Anything electrical will function, its cord apparently plugged in the inside of the hat.*)

JACKIE: If hair is just hair, then why were you always after me about it? Why were you and mom always saying "Can't you do something about your hair?" I HATED that. And now my hair is always the first thing I think about whenever I think about doing anything. Good things, bad things, great things—just running to the store for a quart of milk—I can't think about doing anything without worrying about what I'm going to do with my hair.

PETER: You think about your hair when you think about doing great things?

JACKIE: Yes.

PETER: By great things, you mean—what—curing cancer? Saving children from burning buildings?

JACKIE: Well…yeah. More or less.

PETER: People who do great things don't worry about how great their hair looks while they're doing them.

JACKIE: You never worry about your hair, do you?

PETER: Nope. I'm married now. I worry about Penny's.

ELIZABETH: So. "What doesn't kill you makes you strong" is bullshit. So. I'm an educated woman. Surely I can come up with a way of organizing my thoughts without resorting to a shopworn cliché. After all, as my father-in-law was so very fond of saying: "It's a poor workman who blames his tools. But only an ass would try to blow glass out of his— (*This is a little too crude for her. But—what the hell—*) —asshole."

(*Both toilets flush, and two little old ladies [*JOSEPHINE *and* STELLA*] fling the stall doors open. These are expertly dressed little old ladies—professional old ladies. They're wearing Chanel or Chanel style suits, expensive jewelry, scarves, fabulous handbags, fabulous shoes.*)

STELLA: So I said to him—you cannot undo what you did.

(PETER *dives behind a door, to hide as they burst out of their stalls.* JOSEPHINE *and* STELLA *head for the waiting room area.* STELLA *gives* PETER *a little sideways kick as they pass him. They travel deliberately, perhaps hanging on to each other's arms for support. In some way, they are small tanks. They stride through the waiting room.*)

STELLA: You cannot undo what you did. You gave up that locket.

JOSEPHINE: Frankie's children were whores.

ELIZABETH: This is not happening to me. *(Tries it another way)* This is not happening to me. *(Another way)* This is not happening to me.

STELLA: On his deathbed they squabbled. You could hear them in the next wing.

ELIZABETH: No. It doesn't feel like it's happening to me, but it is. And I don't believe in denial. I just don't.

JOSEPHINE: What those doctors put him through. A crime.

STELLA: So? He came out of it all right, in the end. Surprised 'em all. Of course, he died on the way to Arabia.

(JOSEPHINE and STELLA exit.)

ELIZABETH: This is a nightmare. No, not specific enough. My stomach is on fire, my hands are numb, my heart is beating its brains out, my feet are—where are my feet, they feel like they're in Ohio, were they always all the way down there— *(She snaps back.)* No. A little too specific.

JACKIE: I just don't know how I'm supposed to look for this, Peter. I mean, maybe there is a perfect way to wear your hair while you're in a hospital waiting room, and if I could find it—I mean look at how important hair is to great men and women. Look at Cleopatra. Look at Louis the Fourteenth. How do we recognize them? By their hair. Because their hair was great. So maybe, if I could get my hair absolutely right, I could recognize this.

PETER: Recognize what?

JACKIE: What is happening to me.

PETER: This is not happening to you, it's happening to Dad.

JACKIE: Peter you know what I'm talking about!

PETER: Yeah. Mom's sitting out there alone, and we're in here, talking about hair.

JACKIE: I'm not talking about hair, Peter. I'm talking about greatness.

PETER: Okay. Your hair looks great. So can we go back out now?

(PETER *is headed for the door,* JACKIE *pulls him back.*)

JACKIE: Peter—if I asked you to help me do something—if I really needed your help—would you help me?

PETER: *(Pause)* Sure.

JACKIE: Good.

PETER: So? You going to tell me what you want me to help you do?

JACKIE: Burn it down.

ELIZABETH: I really do need to get this right, I really do. I need a way to—to *name* what is happening to me so I can do it right.

PETER: What are you talking about?

JACKIE: You know what I'm talking about.

PETER: Nope. Don't have a clue.

(NURSE PITKIN *begins putting away all the hair accessories and closing up shop.*)

ELIZABETH: I need a word or a phrase that—that…oh, hell, I just can't— *(Epiphany)* Hell. Yes, of course. That's it! It's obvious! I'm sitting in a three-square foot piece of hell.

(*As* JACKIE *turns, heads into one of the stalls:*)

PETER: Jackie where are you going?

JACKIE: Where does it look like I'm going?

PETER: I don't believe this.

JACKIE: Trust me, Peter. This is one of the easier things to believe.

(JACKIE *goes into the stall, closes the door,* PETER *looks at it, dumbfounded for an instant.*)

NURSE PITKIN: This is just one example of why kidney work was just too limiting for me. (*She puts the top hat away, folds up the shelf, and begins to transform back into* NURSE PITKIN.)

PETER: (*Heading back into the waiting room area. muttering.*) My sister must have the smallest bladder in the world.

NURSE PITKIN: Don't get me wrong. There's nothing wrong with a kidney story. And it's not that kidney work isn't good, fulfilling, honest labor.

PETER: My sister must have a bladder the size of a pea.

NURSE PITKIN: But a kidney story is, in the final dialysis, a lot like a love story. Boy is born with kidney. Boy loses kidney. Boy gets the use of a pseudo kidney. It works out or it doesn't. The end.
I admit I sometimes find myself drawn in by the simple eloquence of a love story—but the sad fact is that the things in me that can be changed by love stories have already been changed.

PETER: I used to feel sorry for Jackie's future husband. I used to imagine her bankrupting him with her toilet paper bills. (*He takes out the Scrabble pad, and begins making computations.*)

NURSE PITKIN: That's why I'm looking for a new story.

PETER: I imagined the headline "WOMAN'S TINY BLADDER BANKRUPTS HUSBAND." And then I met Penny.

ELIZABETH: No, I just can't work with this vague, imprecise "This is hell" shit.

PETER: I married the only other woman in the history of the species. Who also has a bladder the size of a pea.

ELIZABETH: Who the hell knows what hell looks like, right? Hell is just a state of mind. I need to—engage with this thing fully. Otherwise, a person just gets trapped in cheap sentimentality. In bullshit.
And what a person needs at a moment like this is something profound. I need something big, something brutal, something like—

(JACKIE *flushes the toilet. The sound erupts loudly, sounding a bit like an atomic bomb.*)

ELIZABETH: Nagasaki! Yes! Nagasaki fills the bill! Nagasaki—the moment after the blast. The sudden absence of the known world. One moment— everything is fine. Everything is good, or bad, everything is killing or not killing you in ways you can understand. Life is good or bad, but it's there. And then—the next moment—there was no world left. Well, there was a world, but it wasn't any world they knew.

(JACKIE *leaves the bathroom and enters the waiting room area, going to the rack of vending machines. She has a large knapsack with her.* NURSE PITKIN *hides or closes off the interior of the ladies' room.*)

NURSE PITKIN: We are all looking for a new story. Think about it. You know it's true.

ELIZABETH: Yes. Nagasaki. A word that means the absence of the known world will do.

NURSE PITKIN: We thought the bomb was going to be a new story. But in the end, it turned out that death was nothing new. It is a story, however, that contains a small chapter about glass.

(JACKIE *takes a free form green glass object, the color of tourmaline, out of her knapsack.*)

NURSE PITKIN: Glass is basically just sand, and fire. Well, the testing site in New Mexico provided one and the bomb the other.

PETER: At sixty cents a roll, let's say one roll every other day....

NURSE PITKIN: Together they made a lovely green glass, the color of tourmaline. Left it scattered, like a miraculous bloom of emerald Easter eggs, hot and easy to hunt, on the scorched desert floor.

PETER: Three hundred and sixty five divided by two that's one hundred and nine dollars and fifty cents a year.

JACKIE: (*Holds the tourmaline green glass object up into the light*) When I was seven or eight years old, I used to pretend that this was a very rare, very dangerous piece of atom bomb glass.

NURSE PITKIN: Technically speaking, the glass made by the atom bomb would be considered a whimsy, or off-hand glass.

JACKIE: I used to see it, there on the shelf with the other whimsies, and long to touch it.

NURSE PITKIN: Whimsies are pieces of glass that are not made to suit the factory's purpose. They are made after the general run has been completed, made by the workers, in fantastic shapes and shades to show off their skill, and to take home to impress sweethearts and mothers and wives.

JACKIE: I had a whole story I invented about it.

NURSE PITKIN: The scientists at Alamogordo— misplaced craftsmen, to the last—followed this offhand tradition and fashioned jewelry from the choicest bits of glass, harvested from the center of the blast. Their wives wore these pendants and chokers and bracelets proudly. And then their soft skin began to burn beneath the sparkling gemstones. Filled with a fire that lasts.

JACKIE: In the story, this piece of glass has magical radioactive properties that cure the sick, and, at the same time, fits miraculously into a device that defuses every nuclear bomb in existence and ends World War III. *(She puts the green whimsy in an empty compartment in the vending machine.)*

NURSE PITKIN: It was actually made in 1894 by a man named Emanuel Strauss who was the master blower at the Demery Glassworks until about 1933.

JACKIE: Most of my stories end like that. It was my dream, after all. To someday make, with my hands, and my breath, a perfect, world saving piece of glass.

(JACKIE begins pulling more glass objects out of her knapsack—it is necessary to have it rigged as a trick knapsack, so that she can take as many pieces of glass out of it as she needs to. She empties food out of the vending machine—it's one of those types with carousel mechanisms, with lighted windows to display the food—and fills the compartments with beautiful, brilliantly colored glass objects. The light from the vending machines should back-light these "whimsies" beautifully, shinning through, radiating, turning the vending machines into a stained glass window. The vending machines should be scaled larger than normal to make sure the glass objects read properly. Assisting her, NURSE PITKIN hands the glass objects to her.)

ELIZABETH: I know there is something wrong with a woman comparing her husband's surgery to Nagasaki. I am an educated woman. I am aware of the— profanity—involved in borrowing that hideous, unthinkable moment, and transplanting it here.

But I can't help it. And I don't see why I should.
Because the moment that may or may not be the
moment the sudden and absolute absence of the
known world happens to me could happen to me any
moment now.

*(Through the two huge swinging doors that open out of
the place of extreme heat and light, the* OPERATING TEAM
bursts onto the stage.)

OPERATING TEAM: *(They are dressed as All the King's
Horses and All the King's men, with surgical gowns and
caps as well. There should be four of them.* DR GLASS *is at
the head of the parade. They are singing in the best barber
shop harmony.)*
Humpty Dumpty worked like a slave
The family business trying to save
He wore himself down
(Oak Ridge Mountain Boys Bit here:)
Down
Down
Down into bits
And Humpty Dumpty's insides just called it quits

NURSE PITKIN: Enter Doctor Glass and Company.

TEAM: *(Singing)* Humpty Dumpty

DR GLASS: *(Reading from a clipboard)* Pulmonary
function—twenty percent.

TEAM: *(Singing)* Humpty Dumpty

DR GLASS: Blockage of main heart valve—one hundred
percent.

TEAM: *(Singing)* Humpty Dumpty

DR GLASS: Secondary valve blockage—sixty percent

TEAM: *(Singing)* Humpty Dumpty

DR GLASS: Usable cardiac collateral—zip.
Looks like a job for—

DR GLASS & TEAM: *(Singing together)*
All the king's horses
And all the king's men
We'll put Humpty Dumpty
Together again.

DR GLASS: Peter. Good to see you again. *(He shakes his hand enthusiastically, warmly.)*

NURSE PITKIN: Doctor Harold Glass. Yale undergrad. Yale medical. Cholesterol level:

DR GLASS: *(He takes JACKIE's hand.)* And you must be—Jacqueline!

NURSE PITKIN: One hundred fifty-nine.

DR GLASS: Ah! Mrs Demery! *(Shakes ELIZABETH's hand)*

NURSE PITKIN: You can feel it in his handshake—he's got the healing hands.

DR GLASS: We are going in!

ELIZABETH: Oh!

DR GLASS: *(He heartily shakes their hands again, in reverse sequence.)* We're about to begin!

ELIZABETH: Yes?!?

PETER: Look, Doctor Glass, there are still a few questions you never answered that I—

DR GLASS: No time now, son.

(DR GLASS and the TEAM join hands with lightning speed, and in a low tone he invokes:)

DR GLASS: Oh Lord. Give me the skill to do what can be done, the knowledge to know what can't be, and the malpractice insurance to cover them both. Amen.

TEAM: *(Murmurs)* Amen.

(They drop hands, and sing call and response, with DR GLASS singing the lead.)

DR GLASS: We are going in.

TEAM: Going in

DR GLASS: 'Bout to begin!

TEAM: 'Bout to begin

DR GLASS: We are all the king's horses

TEAM: All the king's horses

DR GLASS: We are all the king's men

TEAM: All the king's men.

DR GLASS & TEAM: *(Singing together)*
If anyone can do it
Then we are the men
Who'll put Humpty Dumpty—
Who'll put Humpty Dumpty
Together—again!!!!
AAAAAAAAAGAIN!!!!!!!

(They parade through the revolving doors that lead into the operating room.)

ELIZABETH: Well. That was nice of him, wasn't it? To stop by. To reassure us, like that? So we don't worry? So we know everything's going to be just fine?

JACKIE: I don't trust that doctor.

ELIZABETH: You don't trust anyone, Jackie.

JACKIE: Well why should I?

ELIZABETH: Because you can't go through life not trusting people.

JACKIE: Oh, yes. Let's not forget the Demery Family Golden Rules:
1. Always be overdressed
2. Always stand up for what's right
3. And always trust everyone
That way, we'll be well-dressed, stationary targets who make it easy for people to shoot us down.

ELIZABETH: Jackie—

JACKIE: Peter doesn't trust people either, do you, Peter?

PETER: Hell no. They have to trust me.

JACKIE: See?

ELIZABETH: Don't encourage her, Peter.

PETER: Look, Mom, it's the truth. People have to trust me with their money. Well, you can't give your money to someone you can't trust, and you can't trust a man with your money if he's stupid enough to trust other people, right? It's just a fact of life.

ELIZABETH: Well, it shouldn't be. I can remember when everybody trusted everyone. When the biggest deals were conducted on a simple handshake. Your grandfather never signed a contract in his life. Always said that if his hand on a deal wasn't good enough, it was no deal.

JACKIE: I don't think that's what Granddad used to say Mom. Not exactly.

NURSE PITKIN: I love it when the story dovetails like this. Don't you? The healing hands of business and medicine. Great myths, separately—together like this they—well—they give the new story an old fashioned resonance.

JACKIE: What Granddad used to say, exactly was: "My hands made the glass, and the glass makes the deal, and if my handshake doesn't seal it, then you can kiss my—"

ELIZABETH: Jackie, please.

JACKIE: Well I can't help it, can I? If Granddad loved the word ass. "PEOPLE WHO LIVE IN GLASS HOUSES—

JACKIE & PETER: —GET WATCHED WHILE THEY WIPE THEIR ASS."

(JACKIE *and* PETER *laugh, and* ELIZABETH *sighs and shakes her head.*)

PETER: Boy, he loved the fact that ass rhymed with glass. "What kind of an ass works at the Demery Glass Works?"

JACKIE: "A Demery Ass works at the Demery Glass works—"

PETER: —"at the Demery Glass Works the Demery ass works"—

(Faster, an old game, getting jumbled up)

JACKIE & PETER: "—at the Demery Glass works the Demery ass works the Demery glass at the Demery Glass works the Demery ass works the Demery glass for the ass working glass—"

ELIZABETH: That's enough, you two. *(She's been knitting away, and has finished the row she's working on. She tries to pull up more yarn—it must be stuck—she starts tugging it.)*

NURSE PITKIN: You may be interested to know that we sell Demery Glass, here in the Ladies' Auxiliary Gift Shop, located down the hall, past Pulmonary, take your first right. All proceeds from the gift shop help the Auxiliary purchase the infant car seats— *(She picks up an infant car seat, wrapped in a pink bow, from behind the couch or chair.)* —that we present to each baby born at Saint Mary's. Over twelve hundred given out so far this year.

ELIZABETH: *(She manages to pull more yarn up out of her knitting bag with a nice big tug. The string of yarn—it's a golden brown color—turns into a boa constrictor of approximately the same hue. The boa should be as life-like as possible. She looks at it, continuing to pull up the yarn, transfixed, unbelieving. It begins to wrap itself around her. In a strangled voice as the boa starts to really strangle her.)* Jackie? Peter?

JACKIE: Yeah?

(ELIZABETH *waits for* JACKIE *and* PETER *to notice the snake.*)

PETER: Yeah, Mom?

(ELIZABETH *still waits.*)

PETER: What—is something wrong?

ELIZABETH: *(She realizes they don't see it.)* No. Nothing. What could be wrong? *(She dramatically rips the snake off her, stuffs it and the object she's been knitting back into the bag, and hurriedly pulls out another project, this one made of brightly colored yarn—stripes of red, yellow, and black.)*

NURSE PITKIN: We think of glass as fragile. We are trained, from childhood, to handle it delicately, tenderly, because glass is, first and foremost, a thing that breaks. But technically speaking, glass is forged and fused in fire—which makes it metal. And metal is the last thing we expect to break.

(ELIZABETH *pulls out more yarn. A large coral snake snakes its way out of the bag. She looks at it, looks around her.*)

(JOSEPHINE *and* STELLA *enter from the side of the stage they last exited from. They are played by two different actors. The actors playing them this time may be men, or not.*)

JOSEPHINE: You say she went in for a simple operation?

STELLA: Simple? Simple? Removing a hangnail would of been more complex.

NURSE PITKIN: And there is another secret about glass—a delicious secret, because it seems to be a secret that glass does not know about itself.

JOSEPHINE: They punctured her?

STELLA: Punctured her? Ha. The Hindenberg was just punctured, compared to what they did to her.

JACKIE: Glass is liquid.

STELLA: Like a sieve.

JACKIE: It melts. It flows. *(She takes out a very liquidy formed whimsy.)* That's why you see ripples in old plate glass, and those fat bulges at the bottom of stained glass windows.

STELLA: She was dead when they got her to the table. And she was somewhat worse than that when they were done.

(JOSEPHINE and STELLA have crossed the stage, and gone.)

JACKIE: Glass is nothing more than a kind of ice—room temperature, present tense ice, made of a special water that freezes in time, not cold, and will melt, is melting now.

NURSE PITKIN: Glass begins as sand, becomes a little slow piece of flowing river, and returns to sand. That is the story of glass—sand to sand. It is similar in this respect to the ashes-to-ashes story of the body, but the body's story is always a short one. The story of glass makes a more serious claim upon time.

ELIZABETH: *(Stuffing the coral snake back into the bag)* Well. This is a much more fascinating turn of events than I'd anticipated. But I guess that's the point. *(She pulls out another knitting project—a dark tan one.)* When the known world prepares to absent itself, there's no telling where it prepares to go.

JACKIE: *(Taking out a blue whimsy)* Here is it. The famous Demery Blue. Kinder than cobalt. Colder than turquoise. Oh, you can find glass that looks more or less like this—but nobody else has ever managed to duplicate the exact shade of Demery Blue. *(She puts the blue piece of glass into the vending machine.)* Peter?

PETER: *(Reading The Wall Street Journal)* What?

JACKIE: Don't you ever miss it?

PETER: Miss what?

JACKIE: The glass. Making it.

PETER: I can't believe you're starting in on this, Jackie.

JACKIE: I'd miss it, Peter, I'd miss it—a lot, so I was just wondering, you know, if you missed it, because—

PETER: I CAN'T BELIEVE YOU'RE BRINGING THIS UP AT A TIME LIKE THIS!

JACKIE: All I asked was if you missed making glass, Peter. Jesus.

(A rattlesnake emerges from ELIZABETH's *bag, rattling away.)*

PETER: You just can't pass up an opportunity, can you—give you the smallest opening, you pile up the guilt, you pile on the abuse—

JACKIE: It's a simple question. I can't help it if you feel guilty. I can't help it, and I don't care. It's a simple question, Peter. Do you miss making glass.

PETER: NO.

JACKIE: Thank you.

*(*ELIZABETH *squashes the rattlesnake back in the bag, matter of fact, and takes out a white knitting project.)*

JACKIE: So…how about the abuse? Do you miss that?

PETER: What?

JACKIE: The abuse I always pile on you. Miss that?

PETER: What do you think?

JACKIE: No, I guess not.

NURSE PITKIN: Sometimes, it is necessary to involve one's self more intimately. In a particular family, and their story. We at Saint Mary's are here to help. A thousand C Cs of the three Cs—that's our motto.

(NURSE PITKIN *grabs her* PENNY *costume and holds it in front of her—it is a paper doll cutout version of the evening gown worn in the prologue, except that now it is white. She holds a champagne glass—also identical to the one used in the prologue.)*

JACKIE: After all, if it's abuse you're after, you've got Penny for that.

PETER: *(Stands, flings his* Wall Street Journal *down)* You really are a piece of work, you know that? You really are.

(PETER *turns, without looking where he is going, and runs right into* PENNY/NURSE PITKIN. *He slams into her, crushing the glass between them.)*

PETER: SHIT! PENNY!! You are the last thing I need right now. The very last. *(He stoops down to start picking up the broken bits of glass that have fallen at their feet.)*

ELIZABETH: I suppose a doctor would just call this an anxiety attack. But from where I'm sitting, it sure as hell looks like a cobra to me.

(The white yarn has turned into a huge white king cobra. ELIZABETH *tries to push it back down, business as usual, but it just hisses at her, and rises high and higher.)*

PENNY: Why are you putting that glass in your pocket?

PETER: Go away.

ELIZABETH: What does it eat, what does it eat, it looks hungry. If I could give it something to eat, it might go away.

JACKIE: *(She is about to throw away some food from the vending machines. She reconsiders.)* You want anything, Mom?

ELIZABETH: *(To* JACKIE, *by accident)* A mouse, or a gerbil, maybe—a small rabbit might do the trick.

JACKIE: What Mom?

ELIZABETH: *(Realizing her mistake, covering)* Nothing dear. I'm fine.
I have always considered myself a resourceful woman. It is hard to imagine where a resourceful woman would be hiding the resources to rise to this occasion— but that's the definition of resourceful.

PENNY: *(Watching* PETER *put the shards in his pocket)* I said, why are you putting that glass in your pocket?

PETER: No! I don't want to think about you now. Go away!

PENNY: But you're putting glass in your—

PETER: *(Gives up fighting her appearance)* Yes. I am putting it in my pocket. I put it in my pocket, and you say—

PENNY: That's the stupidest thing I ever saw in my life.

PETER: —and then we get married, and we move three hundred and twenty four miles away from my parents—

PENNY: Breaking your mother's heart.

PETER: —and we have three children, and things go to shit—

PENNY: But we hang on to them anyway.

PETER: —and my father gets sick, and— *(He is still on his knees, at her feet. He starts to weep.)* Tell me you love me, tell me you love me, please tell me you love me.

PENNY: *(Pause)* That's the stupidest thing I ever saw in my life.

(PETER stops weeping, wipes his nose with the back of his hand. Takes visible hold of himself. And continues to pick up the glass fragments, and put them in his pocket.)

PENNY: Well?

ELIZABETH: That P B S special on the Sacred Snakes of India! Yes! I watched that series religiously! They showed this wonderfully grainy black and white film clip of a high priestess, performing an elaborate ritual with a very similar—though much smaller—snake. She had to kiss the snake—peculiar, isn't it, that in a country where it's a crime to touch the majority of the population, it's a blessing to kiss a snake? Anyway, she had to kiss the snake, on its head, three times. Like this. *(She bobs and weaves from side to side along with the movement of the snake, and kisses it.)* That's one.

PENNY: Well, Peter? I said, that's the stupidest—

PETER: I heard you!

PENNY: Then you know what happens next.

PETER: Yeah. *(Ticking it off on his fingers)* Marriage, move, Mom's broken heart, children, shit—

PENNY: Oh, Peter. Don't be coy. You know what happens after you bump into me, spill the champagne and ruin my dress. You know what happens next. *(She drapes herself around his shoulders, from behind.)* Come on. It'll be just like it was, the first time.

(PENNY takes his hands, starts to lead PETER over behind the couch.)

PETER: Here? Now?

ELIZABETH: *(Kisses the snake again)* That's two.

PENNY: Sure. Why not?

PETER: Right here? With my father lying on the operating ta—no, I won't—

PENNY: Sure you will. This is what you need. You know you do.

(PETER turns to PENNY, they embrace passionately, and kiss, and sink down onto the floor, behind the couch.)

ELIZABETH: *(Kissing the snake again)* That's three!

(The snake immediately becomes docile, tame, and it begins to rain.)

ELIZABETH: Rain. Of course! Now I remember.

(It rains only on ELIZABETH. *Sounds of* PETER *and* PENNY *kissing float up from behind the couch.)*

ELIZABETH: The high priestess kisses the cobra for rain.

(The amplified sound of PETER's *zipper being unzipped)*

PENNY: My, oh my!

PETER: —Penny, Penny, please!—

PENNY: Darling you're tearing it—don't tear it—

JACKIE: *(Holding up a beautiful clear and white cased glass object)* This is one of mine.

PENNY: Oh, that tickles. *(She giggles.)*

JACKIE: It's cased glass—two layers of glass, the clear, on the inside, then you pick up a gather of white.

PENNY: *(She giggles some more.)* Stop it stop it stop it stop it!

JACKIE: You work them both and then you grind or carve off parts of the outside so the inside shows.

PENNY: Bad, bad boy.

*(*PENNY *slaps* PETER. *He growls.)*

JACKIE: I was eighteen when I made it.

PETER: —Oh, Jesus, Penny, your skin is so smooth—

JACKIE: I made it to impress a boy named Dickie Shaw.

PENNY: Oh!

PETER: —yes—

PENNY: Now!

PETER: —please—

JACKIE: I don't know where I got the idea that something like this could be a viable part of a mating ritual, but he took one look at it, said, "You really made that?" and asked Sara Toombs to the prom.

ELIZABETH: (Opens her mouth, drinking in the rain) Rain, as it turns out, was the last thing I expected. But I can't really say that I mind. It's quite refreshing. A little warmer than it might be—but I can adapt. I have always prided myself on being an adaptable woman. (She opens the neck of her dress a little, takes out a handkerchief, and gives herself a sponge bath.)

PENNY: Please!

PETER: —now—

PENNY: Yes!

PETER: —oh!—

JACKIE: It turned out that Dickie did ask me out a couple of times after we graduated.

PENNY: Don't stop!

PETER: —I can't stop—

PENNY: Don't stop!

PETER: —I can't—

JACKIE: And after him, there were a half dozen or so serious tries. (She takes out six wildly different whimsies, lines them up on the end table. Then she puts them into the vending machines.)

PENNY: Stay there!

PETER: —I'm trying—

PENNY: Harder! Try there.

ELIZABETH: (Her spit bath well underway, enjoying it) There. I've adapted. I've learned to like it. To use it. To—

(The rain abruptly stops.)

ELIZABETH: Bullshit. Even the rain is full of it.

(Flowers begin to grow around her chair, up out of her knitting bag, and out of her.)

JACKIE: But I just couldn't settle for less. The way Peter did.

ELIZABETH: Flowers. What a nice touch.

PETER: *(His head pops up from behind the couch.)* Jackie I did not settle.

JACKIE: Oh yes you did.

ELIZABETH: Flowers will come in handy, for the hospital room, during recovery, or for the—well, they'll come in handy. Either way.

PENNY: Touch me there!

PETER: —Okay—

PENNY: And there!

PETER: *(Back down behind the couch)* —okay—

PENNY: And there!

PETER: Jackie you're the one that settled.

JACKIE: For what?

ELIZABETH: I do hope they'll be tulips. Tulips would be nice.

PETER: For the glass.

JACKIE: Oh, right. Mister Investment Banker. Mister Man Who Makes Nothing But Money. Mister Man Who Makes Nothing That Stays.

PETER: *(Gasping, out of breath)* Why do you always—

PENNY: AND THERE!!

PETER: —I'm trying!— *(To* JACKIE*)* Why do you always try to make me feel bad about my job, Jackie?

JACKIE: You mean you don't?

(*The flowers are starting to bloom—large, lush, jungle-like.*)

ELIZABETH: Well, they're not tulips.

JACKIE: You mean you like what you do?

PETER: Of course I do—

JACKIE: You like your life?

PETER: I love my children—

JACKIE: Well, who doesn't.

PETER: And my wife—

JACKIE: Sad, but true.

PETER: And my job—

JACKIE:	PENNY/PETER:
You don't have a job, my boyo.	
	YES!
That's the point.	
	GOD!
You are just a conduit.	
	OH!
So that numbers, passing from one bank account to another	
	OH GOD YES
have something to pass through	

(*The flowers continue to bloom—huge, and not tulip-like at all.*)

ELIZABETH:	PENNY/PETER:
No.	
	YES
They're definitely not tulips.	

                                GOD
African violets, maybe.
                                OH
I don't care for violets.
Too showy.
                                YES
But I have to admit
                                OH
they make a lovely corsage.
                                YES—YES—THERE!!!!!!

(PENNY *and* PETER *climax. Appropriate moaning, etc. All the flowers blossom, hideously. All have fang-like teeth, and scalpel like incisors.* ELIZABETH *reaches out, and picks one of the flowers. It bites her. She screams.*)

JACKIE: (*Rushing to her mother's side*) What's wrong!

(*But* JACKIE *is interrupted by the revolving door thundering into motion. It is a terrifying, huge sound.*)

THE SINGING TELEGRAM : (*Dressed in equal parts surgical garb and singing telegram uniform, the singing telegram deliverer emerges from the revolving doors, after several terrifying revolutions, singing:*)
Singing Telegram for the Demerys
Singing the Demery Telegram
(*He/She is up to the area where the family is. Spoken:*) You the Demerys?

(*All three nod, struck dumb with terror at what they may hear.*)

THE SINGING TELEGRAM : (*Sung:*)
They're in. They're in!
His system stood up beautifully
to the trauma of the drama of the opening
And I've been sent to tell the tale
to report the patient hearty and hale
and chances are his heart won't fail!
(*Spoken aside*) during the next seven hours of the

operation
SO!
(He/she breaks into one of those show tune finale type dance kicks.)
That's all for now
No more to say
I hope I was clear
I know that you are
just sick with fear
but that's all for now
no more to say
sign here...

(JACKIE, ELIZABETH, and PETER just look at him/her numbly, mouths open, uncomprehending. THE SINGING TELEGRAM looks at them all expectantly, holding out the form on the clipboard for them to sign.)

PENNY: *(Hissing)* Peter. PETER!!

(PETER rouses himself, stands, quickly pulling up his pants, takes the clipboard, signs for the telegram. THE SINGING TELEGRAM puts out his/her hand out for a tip. PETER fishes into his pocket, gives him/her one. He/she taps off.)

NURSE PITKIN: *(She is putting on her cap, getting back into her efficient NURSE PITKIN persona.)* I don't want you all to think I indulge myself often like that. I don't. Get too involved, and a story nurse loses her perspective. Her point of view. Still, a good story nurse does her best to straddle both worlds. To acquaint herself— intimately—with the hospital narrative from both sides of the story line.

JACKIE: Thank God. The hard part's over.

ELIZABETH: *(She stares at the place where the flower bit her. She is in shock.)* Poisoned.

PETER: See, Mom. It's all going to be okay.

ELIZABETH: *(She is rocking in her chair, back and forth.)* I should have expected the bite. I should have expected the venom. The sting. The pain.

JACKIE: The hard parts getting in, and now that that's over, Dad should be—Mom—Mom? You okay?

ELIZABETH: And I'm cold. So cold.

JACKIE: Mom—MOM!

ELIZABETH: What, dear?

JACKIE: Are you okay?

ELIZABETH: Of course I'm okay. Why wouldn't I be? *(To herself again, keening, rocking)* This is the way the world ends. This is the way the world ends. *(Screaming)* THE GODDAMN FUCKERS LIED TO ME ABOUT THE WAY THE WORLD ENDS! THEY LIED ABOUT THE WHIMPER! THEY LIED ABOUT THE BITE! THEY NEVER MENTIONED THE POISON!
Damn. Now I've used up the word fuck. I've used the word fuck, and it's just the beginning. Just the first hour. When it gets to be hour number five, number seven—what am I going to have left?

(JACKIE and PETER are looking at ELIZABETH, worried:)

JACKIE: Would you like us to get you something to eat? A cup of coffee, that might make you feel better?

ELIZABETH: *(Sweetly)* No, no, I'm fine. Perfectly fine.

PETER: You sure, Mom? You look kind of funny.

ELIZABETH: What do you mean, is there something wrong with the way I look—

JACKIE: No, no, of course there isn't— *(To PETER)* What is the matter with you?

PETER: What? What?

ELIZABETH: I don't suppose that windbag Socrates gave his appearance a second thought, as the poison from that hemlock cocktail worked its way north, up through his body.

JACKIE: You don't tell a woman she looks funny. Funny—tired—upset—you never tell her.

PETER: But Jackie—

ELIZABETH: Cleopatra, on the other hand, probably didn't think about anything else *except* the way she looked. Of course, she took the asp express—ten to twenty seconds from take off to arrival—which gave her little time, it's true for philosophical or cosmetic contemplation.

PETER: But she does look funny—

ELIZABETH: Obviously I have my choice of traditions. And, even while it seems deeply superficial to be concerned with how I look at a time like this—I have a responsibility to the children. So—for their sakes— *(She begins straightening her hair, her dress, the flowers growing out of her and the chair. To* PETER *and* JACKIE*)* I know I must look a little worried. After all, I *am* worried. I'm supposed to look worried.

PETER: *(Lying)* Mom, you look fine. *(He kisses her cheek, and lies better.)* You look fine even when you're worried.

(NURSE PITKIN *takes out gardening cum surgical instruments, and begins to do a little gardening on* ELIZABETH *and her flowers.)*

ELIZABETH: It's just…it's just that I was thinking about the sound it makes.

JACKIE: The sound what makes?

ELIZABETH: You know. The sound it makes when—you know. When they take your father and they uncover his chest and they…they cr… *(She can't say the word, because it doesn't make sense.)*

NURSE PITKIN: *(To the rescue. She says the word crack for her.)* Crack—to decode, decipher, or decrypt.

ELIZABETH: *(She's trying to say it, but—)* …when they cr…

NURSE PITKIN: Crack—a joke, drollery, gag, or jest.

ELIZABETH: …open his…when they cr…

NURSE PITKIN: Crack—to do in an instant, a jiffy, a flash—in the space of a twinkling wink of an eye.

ELIZABETH: …when they cr… *(She is getting increasingly distressed about this.)*

NURSE PITKIN: Crack—proficient at, cracker jack, masterful, expert, skilled.

ELIZABETH: …open his…Jackie? I can't—I can't—

NURSE PITKIN: Crack—take a stab at, a shot at, a whack at, a whirl.

JACKIE: What, Mom, what is it—

ELIZABETH: When they—when they—

ELIZABETH/NURSE PITKIN: *(*NURSE PITKIN *a definition delivery,* ELIZABETH *feeling every syllable of pain.)* Smash and splinter and carve and split and rend and shatter and slice and—

JACKIE: Mom, what—what—

ELIZABETH/PITKIN: *(*ELIZABETH *exploding with it.)* —and slash and gut and spill and—

JACKIE: Mom, Mom, are you okay—MOM!!

ELIZABETH: Oh. I'm sorry, Jackie. *(Very rationally, calmly)* I was just wondering what it sounded like, when they cr—when they opened him up.

JACKIE: Let's talk about something else, okay? Get your mind off it.

PETER: Jackie, she wants to talk about it, let's talk about it.

(JACKIE *yanks* PETER *to the side for a little chat.*)

JACKIE: This is the absolute last thing she should be thinking about.

PETER: Who made you the expert all of a sudden?

ELIZABETH: Everything is so cold. Everything is so slow. And thin. And far away. How did the world get so thin? And slow? And cold.

(JOSEPHINE *and* STELLA *enter. They are played by two other actors, wearing the Stella and Josephine costumes.* STELLA *is carrying a tray with glasses of orange, tomato, and apple juice on it. Both of them are wearing large orange buttons with the slogan* "SAINT MARY'S JUICES FOR YOU!" *written on them.*)

JOSEPHINE: Well, he got up in the middle of the night to go to the bathroom after that little operation to remove that growth on his nose. Broke his leg.

PETER: Do me a favor, Jackie. (*He is still disheveled from his tryst behind the couch. He reknots his tie, straightens himself up, taking his time.*)

JOSEPHINE: When they were setting the leg, they noticed he'd formed a clot.

PETER: Let me talk to mom the way I want to? And stop nagging me about the glass.

JOSEPHINE: Well, the medication they gave him to break up the clot started him hemorrhaging.

PETER: It upsets her. You know it does.

JOSEPHINE: They gave him something to stop the hemorrhage.

JACKIE: Oh—so now I don't have your permission to talk about glass, is that it? I can't even MENTION the word?

JOSEPHINE: Meanwhile, the clot broke up, lodged in his brain, he had a stroke. *(She offers them a glass of juice from the tray.)*

JACKIE: Well here's a news bulletin, Peter—I'll say the word glass all I want to. *(She takes a glass of apple juice off the tray, drains it down.)*

JOSEPHINE: He survived the stroke, the operation to reverse it, and the post-op trauma, but—he had an adverse to the anesthesia. Puffed right up.

JACKIE: *(Holding up her empty glass, checking the touch mark on the bottom)* Demery Glass. See? I said the word glass again. *(She puts the glass down on the tray, and returns to the vending machines.)*

JOSEPHINE: Well, he developed a bad bladder infection from the medication they gave him to puff him down—had to catheterize him, the tip broke off. Bam. Back to surgery. Pre-op thought he was a Mister E Brown, not Mister F Brown. And that's why they gave him the proctoscope. By mistake.

STELLA: And that's when they found the cancer?

JOSEPHINE: Yep. *(She puts the tray of juice glasses down on the coffee table.)* And just in the nick of time, too.

PETER: Mom?

ELIZABETH: Yes dear?

PETER: What do you say we take a little walk, maybe go down to the cafeteria—

ELIZABETH: All right, dear. That might be nice— *(She tries to stand, but her legs are entwined, prisoners of the vines and flowers.)* Actually, Peter—I'd just as soon not. If that's all right?

PETER: Sure it's all right. We can just say here and talk, all right?

ELIZABETH: All right.

PETER: Now. About that sound.

ELIZABETH: No, Jackie's right. We shouldn't talk about it.

PETER: But we should. Just in a different way. The way we should talk about that sound is—as sounding good.

ELIZABETH: *(Looks at him as if he's from the planet Mars)* Good?

JACKIE: *(Putting more whimsies in the vending machine)* Here's an interesting piece. From an order of custom bottles for General Grant during the Civil war.

PETER: See, we're looking at it as something horrible, but to the doctors, that sound is just a part of their job.

JACKIE: Has a hidden chamber in it. Looks empty, but it's really half full. *(She puts her head back, and tosses some liquid down her throat to demonstrate.)*

PETER: I figure there's one way it sounds, when they do it right, and another way, when they do it wrong. And since these doctors are the best—I made it my job to make sure that the absolute best is what they are—then the sound is not just good, it's the absolute best it can be.

NURSE PITKIN: *(Taking a break from gardening, she sits back on her heels, wipes her brow.)* Nobody ever had to tell the Demery Twins that glass was good. It was obvious to them, at every turn, that the glass their family made was the most durable substance in the world.

PETER: Can you think about it like that? Can you do that, Mom?

(ELIZABETH *hugs* PETER *to her as tightly as she can, with her flower covered arms.*)

ELIZABETH: *(Over his shoulder, to herself)* My son thinks I'm an idiot.

NURSE PITKIN: Their name was Demery, but in a town built on glass, they were known to everyone as the glass twins.

ELIZABETH: He's sweet, and wonderful, and he thinks his mother is an idiot. *(She kisses him on the top of his head.)* His wife thinks so too. Well, maybe she's right. Maybe she's—well of course! That's it! I'll be an idiot!

NURSE PITKIN: They were made from the finest, purest sand in the world—the famous Crystal City sand, the silica of dreams. And they would flow, perhaps, one day, back into the ground, melting gracefully, in the pull of time, like all good glass. But breaking, in any way, shape, or form, was out of the question.

ELIZABETH: Since being strong and and organized and resourceful and adaptable hasn't done me a damn bit of good—I'll be an idiot. I'll give up fighting to be strong, to get on top of this. I'll let it get on top of me. Thank you, Peter. I will try to think about everything that's…going on in there as good. *(She kisses him again, and lets him go.)* It's such a relief to be an idiot. I don't know why I didn't think of it before.

NURSE PITKIN: *(Picks up a fragment of glass from* PENNY'*s broken champagne glass)* Saint Mary's is also a story built on glass. Most of our oldest hospitals are. In America—a land built on hard work—the first work was glass. Even before the Jamestown settlers had food to eat or huts to sleep in, they built a small glass works, for the production of glass beads, for trade with the Indians. Consequently, among the settlement's first recorded injuries and deaths, are those involving accidents that occurred during the manufacture of glass. It is no coincidence that the Glass Works is so convenient to the hospital. The story of hospitals and the story of glass have always gone hand in hand. *(She draws the shard across the palm of her hand. A line of deep red blood appears.)*

(PETER *sees what* JACKIE *is doing at the vending machines:)*

PETER: Jesus Christ—what the hell do you think you're doing! *(He rushes back.)* Goddamn it, Penny—

JACKIE: Penny? I hate it when you call me Penny.

(NURSE PITKIN *has moved to a pre-set medical kit, and removes a piece of gauze.)*

ELIZABETH: Well now. Let's see. What would an idiot be thinking about at a time like this.

PETER: You can't do this—they're all we've got left.

JACKIE: Wrong-o. I'm getting rid of them—so they're semi-left. At best.

PETER: This is crazy.

JACKIE: It's not my fault Granddad left you and Dad the works. And left all the glass to me.

(PETER *begins fishing around for some change in his pocket, to buy back some of the whimsies.)*

NURSE PITKIN: *(Bandaging her hand)* Glass work was so hard on the men who gave the glass that for two hundred years, not a single glass house in America stayed in continuous operation for longer than five years.

PETER: They're mine just as much as they are yours— no matter what Granddad did—

JACKIE: Wrong-o again. But—I'm prepared to make you a deal. I am prepared to sell you my birthright. I am prepared to trade you. My birthright—for yours.

(The entire upstage wall is now an entire wall of glass objects in the vending machine shelves.)

NURSE PITKIN: If the works didn't burn down, or the workers didn't strike, or the insatiable furnaces didn't reduce every available stand of timber within a hundred miles to mud and stumps—the glass works simply ran out of men. Or rather—used them up. Broke them, from the inside out. In the small sun heat of the crucible, their hearts exploded in their chests. Their lungs, coated with whisper fine silica dust, aching from the strain of pushing breath into molten metal, gave out, and gave out, and gave out.

ELIZABETH: Well, I might be worrying about whether I left the tea kettle on, or turned the iron off, but I wasn't an idiot when I left the house this morning, so I really can't justify worrying about that.

PETER: Tomorrow morning, when Dad's fine, and you've returned to the planet, you are really going to hate yourself for doing this.

JACKIE: No I'm not.

PETER: All right, then. *I'll* hate you.

ELIZABETH: Can't think about now. Can't think about later. Well, that leaves—before. Yes—I think that's just what an idiot would think about at a time like this— they'd think about their life *before* the known world announced its intention to just up and vanish—they'd think about the world when it was still whole.

JACKIE: *(As she puts a purple piece of glass in the vending machine.)* Look, Peter. It's Granddad's heart.

(The door slides shut on it. She gets out some change, drops it in, and retrieves the purple glass piece.)

JACKIE: The last piece of glass he made. *(She holds it up to the light.)* Granddad's purple heart. I mean, it's not like it's this piece that killed him, you know, not really, that's cockeyed thinking, but the human race will romanticize things like this, like it's the bullet and not the war that kills a man, you know. I think it's because a bullet is easier to hold in your hand than a war.

PETER: Do you have any idea what a collector would give you for these?

JACKIE: Yeah. Money. Amazing, isn't it? How can that be right? That money—piles and piles of money is the only thing you can get for these. *(She gives* PETER *a handful of change.)* Here's the deal: Pick one. Pick any one you like. It's yours—no matter what happens, it's yours to keep. I'll give it to you free, and clear. But if I can guess the one you pick—you win them all. Only one catch. I get the works, in return. It's a trade. You get the glass, I get the works. Oh, actually, there are two catches—you have to come with me, and you have to—I guess there are three catches. You have to help me too. That's the deal.

PETER: Help you do what?

JACKIE: Is it a deal?

PETER: No, it's not a deal. What do I get if you guess wrong?

JACKIE: I won't guess wrong.

PETER: Of course you won't. You'll cheat.

JACKIE: I know you better than anyone in the world, Peter, I don't need to cheat. I know which one you'll pick.

PETER: Say I agree to do this. Say I pick one. Say you guess right. Say I go with you—

NURSE PITKIN: *(Comes downstage, and in her best stage whisper says:)* This is a simple story.

PETER: What happens next?

NURSE PITKIN: I believe in stylistic simplicity. At the beginning of the course of any disease, the scenario is always simple.
S-I-M-P-L-E.
Lips smile,
plies,
impels slime,
limp lies.

JACKIE: It's just a phone call, right? A dial tone. Seven numbers. Some man's voice, on the other end. A simple phone call. And it's all gone.

NURSE PITKIN: In the beginning, the scenario is always simple. It is only later that complications set in.

PETER: You're not serious.

JACKIE: I am.

NURSE PITKIN: Simple story…going once…

PETER: This is a joke.

JACKIE: Yeah. On us.

NURSE PITKIN: Going twice…

PETER: Look, Jackie— *(He looks longingly at the whimsies trapped in the vending machines.)* —you want to throw these away—it's crazy, it's hurtful, it's mean, irrational, but doing that—that other thing…you've got no right to do it, Jackie. No right at all. The glass is yours. All the glass. Past, present, and future. The glass is yours. But the works. Are mine.

JACKIE: Funny guy, Grandpa. To do that.

PETER: Yeah. Funny guy.

JACKIE: I don't want to do it alone, Peter.

PETER: Do it—I can't even believe we're talking about it!

JACKIE: Yeah. I'd much rather burn it down. Return it to the fire. That's what Granddad would say. Return it to the asshole fire. From whence it came.

NURSE PITKIN: In the drop of molten glass that falls, unnoticed, into the packing material. In the escaping spark from the roaring furnace. In the exploding shard from a flawed, red-hot flask. The fire is always waiting. Fire, the glass man's greatest fear, is always there, waiting. To take back everything it gives.

JACKIE: I need you. What'd Granddad always say? Takes two to light the asshole furnace. One to hold the light, and one to watch out for the arms of the fire. The greedy, asshole fire.

PETER: I will not help you make that phone call! I won't do it.

JACKIE: Yes you will. You want these whimsies, don't you? So you will.

PETER: What if I need it to say, Jackie? What if I need some place—that stays?

JACKIE: To come back to?

PETER: You know I can't come back—you know Penny, you know she'd never—Jackie, I think she'd leave me if I—you know I can't come back.

NURSE PITKIN: A simple story going once—twice—three times.

JACKIE: (Shrugs) Then it's gone already. If you're not coming back—it's already gone.

NURSE PITKIN: A simple story—gone.

PETER: But what about Dad—what about—

JACKIE: You heard Mom last night.

ELIZABETH: I don't know why I'm torturing myself like this. It's really very simple. I'll just think about when I was young, and nothing bad had ever happened to me, or ever would.

PETER: Yeah.

JACKIE: She meant it.

PETER: She didn't mean this.

JACKIE: It doesn't matter what she meant. He promised her. He never sets foot in the Demery Glass Works again.

ELIZABETH: I'll think about the day I met him. How strong and handsome he looked. And nothing bad had ever happened to him, or ever would.

(PETER *plays with the coins in his hand for a moment.*)

ELIZABETH: I'll start with him walking toward me. From far down the street. I'm visiting my cousin, Betty, and I look up, and there's a man, walking toward me. I can't quite see his face.

(JACKIE *turns her back on* PETER, *so she won't be able to see which whimsey he picks. He puts in the money, and selects a goblet—Nile blue, partially cased in ruby glass, a magnificent goblet with ropes and swirls—heavy and delicate, at the same time.*)

JACKIE: Got it?

PETER: Got it.

ELIZABETH: I watch him coming toward me. I like the way he walks. I turn to Betty and I say, "I like the way he walks." And Betty says, "That's Victor Demery." And I say, "Who's that?" And she says, "Everybody knows who the Demery's are."

JACKIE: You've picked Red Demery's Egyptian Goblet—presented to his wife, our great-great-great-great grandmother Louise upon the birth of their first son, Peter MacDowell Demery. January 17, 1810. The

King's Cup. *(She turns, sees that she's guessed correctly.)*
Let's go.

PETER: But I thought they were mine now—

JACKIE: Not until after—

PETER: But what if somebody takes them—we can't just
leave them here like this!

JACKIE: Why not? Because they're beautiful? Because
they're history? Because they're ours?

PETER: Yes.

JACKIE: No. Because they're beautiful, and historical,
and ours. That's why I have to leave them. I have to,
Peter. I have to leave them all behind.

(NURSE PITKIN hands JACKIE another glass object.)

JACKIE: You ever destroyed anything beautiful?
No? Me either. The perfect glass twins never had a
destructive impulse in their lives.

NURSE PITKIN: Something truly lovely—to hold it in
your hand—to feel the weight of it, the work in it,
the care, the spirit of the maker, the special—oh, the
Japanese have a word for it, Wu or Li, my notes, it
seems, are not precise on this—a small word—for
the being of the object—made in harmony. To hold
something lovely in your hand, and feel the Wu, or the
Li, completely—and then—

*(JACKIE smashes the glass piece she is holding against the
side of the vending machine. PETER moves to stop her, too
late.)*

JACKIE: This is not the kind of thing a Demery does, of
course.

*(PETER stoops down and begins picking up the broken glass
and putting it in his pocket.)*

JACKIE: Believe me, I know that. I am well aware. A Demery does not ever destroy something beautiful. The Demerys prefer to let something beautiful destroy them.

ELIZABETH: I'm going to just stand here, waiting. *(She smiles.)* It's a beautiful day, and I can't think of a better place to wait.

JACKIE: Let's go. *(She goes over to* ELIZABETH.*)* Mom?

ELIZABETH: *(Calm, serene)* Yes, dear?

JACKIE: You all right? You need anything?

ELIZABETH: Not a thing, darling.

JACKIE: You're sure? Because Peter and I, we thought we'd take a little walk. Stretch our legs.

ELIZABETH: A walk? What a good idea. It's such a beautiful day. You go on, I'll stay here.

JACKIE: You sure you'll be okay?

ELIZABETH: I'm perfectly fine.

*(*JACKIE *kisses her.* PETER *gets up from picking up the glass, kisses her too.)*

JACKIE: We won't be long.

ELIZABETH: Yes. He's walking toward me, on his long, strong legs. I can see his face now. He's almost here.

(As JACKIE *passes by the coffee table, she notices the Scrabble board.)*

JACKIE: Glass. G-L-A-S-S. Eight points. Triple word score. Twenty four. *(She scoops up the letters.)* You made glass, Peter. What do you know.

*(*JACKIE *puts them in her pocket, as* PETER *puts the shards of glass in his.)*

JACKIE: For the last time. A Demery made glass.

(They move toward the doors that lead to a place of great heat and light. As they go through the doors, the hospital waiting room walls begin to roll down, revealing the operating theater, which takes up most of the stage.)

(DR GLASS and the TEAM are dressed as part surgeons, part heavily romanticized boatmen. They toil over the body on the table which in some way is a barge on a canal. They are bailing, and singing in lusty full-throated harmony.)

DR GLASS: I feel just like
That guy LaSalle

TEAM: Five C Cs from the ventral canal

DR GLASS: I'm exploring deep into every valve

TEAM: Five C Cs from the ventral canal

DR GLASS: We've cleaned some clogged veins
In our day
Filled with plaque
Blocked by decay
And every inch of the way we know
From the a-or-ta
To the chambers be-low…oh…
Suction—everybody now!

DR GLASS & TEAM:
Suction—suck out all that blood and bile
Cause the body is a Venice
Sinking fast, you know that now
If you've ever navigated on
The ventral canal

(Lights fade on the operating theater.)

(Blackout)

END OF PART ONE

PART TWO

(Lights up on NURSE PITKIN, *helping with the final set change for PART TWO.)*

NURSE PITKIN: You know, sometimes patients ask me what's it like to be a Story Nurse. Nurse Pitkin, they say, how exactly do you manage to administer to a story? Well, I tell them, every story starts and ends, in a body.

*(*VICTOR DEMERY *emerges from the operating theater area, in a sort of fog, literal and figurative. He is naked, except for a loud Hawaiian shirt. He is still attached to the operating table by tubes and wires, poking out from under his shirt, taped to his arms, etc.* NURSE PITKIN *strides across the stage to assist him.)*

NURSE PITKIN: Allow me to introduce Victor Demery, the body of our story. *(She helps him walk.)* Now it's gotten very popular, lately, in hospital stories, to portray the body as a machine—referring to the heart as a hydraulic pump, the lungs as a kind of sophisticated air conditioner, the brain and nervous system as an on-board computer of miraculous complexity and design. And frankly, this kind of thinking is not unknown to my profession—we cover it all, in Story Nursing 101.

*(*VICTOR *goes over to* ELIZABETH, *perched on her miniaturized chair, encased in flowers, knitting. He is still "on the table," floating in the sub-dream world of anesthesia.*

*He shows every emotion completely on his face the instant
he feels it—it washes over him, uncensored. His presence is
childlike, in a peaceful, calm, trusting way.* ELIZABETH *looks
up, sees him coming toward her.)*

ELIZABETH: There you are, dear. I was just thinking
about you. *(She pats the seat next to her, indicating he
should sit. She helps him adjust his tubes and wires, making
him comfortable.)*

NURSE PITKIN: But our advanced training concentrates
on one thing. On the genetic need for story. For a
story that binds up the gaps and holes and mechanical
glitches of the body, and makes it true, and coherent,
and strong.

ELIZABETH: So. What's your day been like so far?

VICTOR: *(At first he finds it difficult to find the words, he
searches for them somewhere deep inside him.)* Mostly…
mostly dreams…dreams I can't…quite hold on to.
Then it was…water. Deep blue green water. A stacked
sea of water, sheets and sheets of it—count backwards
from one hundred, ninety-nine, ninety-eight, ninety-
seven…waves come in sevens. CRASSssshhhhh so
soft. Glass water, water glass, lots of water. *(He smiles.)*
Waikiki Beach.

ELIZABETH: Oh, I am sorry about the shirt—but I just
can't bear to think about what's happening to you
under it.

VICTOR: It is a bit—loud—

ELIZABETH: All right, then I'll think about you wearing
something less flashy—

(NURSE PITKIN whips out a jacket and tie.)

VICTOR: No. No. Shirt's fine.

*(VICTOR shakes his head. NURSE PITKIN disposes of the
clothing.)*

(Lights up on the operating theater/glass works, as JACKIE *and* PETER *enter, through the great doors leading "into a place of great heat and light" which, since the set switch, have been placed on an upstage wall.* JACKIE *takes off her shoes and rubs her feet.)*

JACKIE: My feet hurt.

PETER: You shouldn't have worn those shoes.

JACKIE: I know, I know. But you know Mom. She'd expect me to overdress for the end of the world.

ELIZABETH: So. What are you dreaming about now?

VICTOR: Chips. The cocker spaniel I had when I was a kid.

ELIZABETH: That's nice. I've been thinking about our honeymoon. Niagara Falls. I was thinking about Nagasaki, earlier. Nagasaki. Niagara. Well, at least I'm getting around.

JACKIE: Running shoes! Why didn't I wear my running shoes?

*(*JOSEPHINE *and* STELLA *enter, played by different actors.)*

STELLA: So I said, "Doctor, Doctor, I have this pain" I said. "Do you have normal bowel movements?" the doctor said. "Yes" I said. He nodded his head.

JACKIE: There is almost nothing bad that happens to you where you wouldn't be better off wearing running shoes.

STELLA: So then I decided to ask him. I decided—what the hell. I asked.

JOSEPHINE: You didn't.

STELLA: I did. I said, "What's normal, Doctor?" That's what I said.

JACKIE: Even the end of the world would be better—if the bomb falls, let me be wearing my Nikes.

STELLA: Well, he said. Abnormal bowel movements are ridged. Or spotted. Or very thin. Or very hard. Or very loose. Or very long. Or green. Or red. Or golden. Unless, of course, they're always ridged. Or spotted. Or thin or hard or loose or long or green or red or gold. It turns out, Josephine, that doctors have no idea what a normal bowel movement is. They pretend they do. But bowel movements are like snowflakes. Each one is different. No two are alike. In all the universe, there never has been, and there never will be, two that are the same.

(JOSEPHINE *and* STELLA *exit.*)

VICTOR: He…he…he's all the wrong color!

ELIZABETH: Who is, dear?

VICTOR: Chips. He's…orange.

ELIZABETH: (*Putting down her knitting, preparing to get up.*) Would you like me to speak to the anesthesiologist? Maybe a little different mixture, a lighter hand on the gas—

VICTOR: No. He looks okay orange.

ELIZABETH: He does?

VICTOR: Yes.

ELIZABETH: Well. If you're sure. (*She goes back to knitting.*)

PETER: (*Looking around the works/operating theater*) It's funny, you know? You'd think I'd think about dad—or Granddad at least—but whenever I come here—

JACKIE: You never come here.

PETER: Whenever I come here, I always think of Mackie first. (*He sits down in the master's chair.*)

(DR GLASS *and the operating* TEAM *are all dressed as part surgeons, part as glass workers in the Demery Glass Works*

in the 1960s. Every man is holding, or has ready access to a
large glass pitkin of beer. The operating table/furnace is the
center of the activity.)

DR GLASS/MACKIE: Look who's here boys—Peter my
bucko—Jackie my pearl!

JACKIE: Mackie!

(He sweeps her up in his arms.)

MACKIE: You're just in time! We're relighting old
Archimedes today!

NURSE PITKIN: Most glassmen named their center
furnaces after their wives. Cynthia. Annabell. Sue. Not
the Demerys. King Soloman. King Midas. Archimedes.
The Demerys chose names that acknowledged the
everyday alchemy that transformed sand and fire into
gold.

PETER: How is Mackie doing, anyway?

JACKIE: He died. Last year.

MACKIE: Joe. Stu? What are you fine fellows doing
standing around? You think a furnace can load and
light itself? Get at it.

(They return to the table, and load the fuel into the furnace.)

PETER: He died?

JACKIE: Oh come on, Peter, he was ninety-three years
old.

PETER: I just can't believe someone didn't tell me.

JACKIE: Why? You wouldn't have come home for the
funeral, would you?

PETER: No, but—

ELIZABETH: I can't go on without you, you know.

VICTOR: Lizbeth—

ELIZABETH: No, I know what you're going to say, but I just can't. I absolutely can't. Everybody expects me to be a tower of strength, a Rock of Gibraltar, a regular Hercules of grief, just shoulder the load and go on like Jackie O but I won't. It's a lot harder not going on. People think it isn't, but it is. It's much harder letting it break you. In fact, it seems to be the hardest thing in the world to actually do.

(*As* STU *starts to light the furnace with a long match:*)

MACKIE: Stu—what the hell you doing!

(STU *pulls back.*)

STU: Lighting—lighting the furnace?

MACKIE: He's lighting the furnace! Boys, he's lighting old Archimedes without waiting for me to throw one to the sandman!

CLINT: Oh, shit—

JOE: Jesus, Stu, don't you know what that means?

CLINT: It means Mackie's gonna tell that damn story again.

MACKIE: (*Has been searching around in the cullet, finds a bottle.*) Here we go boys—no, no. (*He throws it back, resumes searching.*) Had a chip. Nothing but the best for the sandman.

NURSE PITKIN: Nothing but the best for the sandman. The ghost who haunts the Demery glassworks. A central figure in the private mythology that has been passed from worker to worker, father to son.

MACKIE: (*He finds another bottle.*) Ah. That's more like it. Not a flaw. Not a bubble. Not a scratch. Ready?

JOE/STU/CLINT/JACKIE : Ready.

MACKIE: (*Positions himself in front of the furnace/operating table.*) One for the sandman! (*And throws it. It breaks.*)

Ah, well. I have the feeling he'll catch it next time. Stu—go ahead with that dangerous match of yours. Clint, watch for sparks.

(STU *approaches the furnace.*)

STU: Clint?

(CLINT *nods, watching.* STU *strikes a long match, and lights the furnace. He turns a small valve.*)

STU: Valve to one quarter.

(PETER *starts picking through the piles of broken glass.*)

JACKIE: *(Watching him)* What are you doing, Peter?

PETER: One for the sandman.

JACKIE: Forget it. Everything's been picked over—the neighbor kids have been in here, climbing around since we shut down—

PETER: *(Holds up a small white plate)* How about this one? Seems okay—

JACKIE: Milk glass? Milk glass is an insult. No light. No soul.

(PETER *tosses it away.* JACKIE *joins him in picking through a pile of cullet and operating room instruments in the corner.*)

STU: Valve to one half.

(*The fire grows in intensity.*)

JACKIE: *(Holding up a small vase)* Look, Peter, I found— oh, shit. Has a crack. *(She throws it back on the pile.)* Just a small one. But I have never believed in anything but the best for the sandman, whether I believed in him or not.

PETER: That's typical Jackie thinking.

STU: Three quarters open.

PETER: *(Looking around some more)* You should have let me keep that plate, Jackie, I'm not finding anything.

JACKIE: Either there's one for the sandman, or there isn't, bucko.

PETER: Okay, okay.

STU: Full open. Furnace is set.

(The furnace roars as it flares to maximum.)

JACKIE: *(Holding up a piece of a vase that is a flesh-colored pink.)* Look, Peter—Granddad's favorite color: *(Imitating her grandfather's voice.)* Rosy Fingered Dawn to the Buying Public—

JACKIE/PETER: But ASSHOLE, to those in the know.

JACKIE: Granddad always came up with the best names for his colors.

PETER: Here's Mackie's favorite. *(He holds up a large piece of a brown-tinted liquor bottle.)*

JACKIE/PETER: Anything rye whiskey comes in.

MACKIE: Peter! PEEEEE-TERRRRR!! We're dry! Fetch the men their beers! Gather round, boys, I don't want nobody complaining they can't hear.

(NURSE PITKIN carries a tray of beer filled clear or bottle green pitkins around to MACKIE and the glassworkers. They each take one, and drink.)

CLINT: Oh, Jesus Mackie, do you have to tell it again.

MACKIE: Listen to him bellyache! Like listening to a story's gonna hurt him.

NURSE PITKIN: Near the end of his life, Lester Mack needed to believe his own stories. He began to relive his imaginary encounters with the sandman, convinced that they had truly happened. They were a great comfort to him.

MACKIE: "Well, the first shot had barely been fired at Fort Sumter, when the works was flooded with orders."

JOE: Mackie, we've all heard it twenty times, already—

MACKIE: Shut up and listen, I might tell it different this time. "Now they say an army marches on its stomach, but there's more than hardtack and beans in there. There's whiskey! And when an army needs whiskey, it needs bottles to put it in. Shifts was doubled, then tripled, and still they couldn't put the bottles out fast enough. Furnaces were going, full blast, twenty-four hours a day. And they say the heat was so fierce, for a mile in ever' direction, the grass withered up and the cows all went dry."

(The glassworkers all moo.)

MACKIE: "An' in the works proper, why the men couldn't see more'n a foot in front of their faces. There was a dust storm raging there, day and night, a dust storm that was one part sand, one part flux, and one hundred percent heat."

(The glassworkers all chime in on the word heat, after all, they know every word by heart.)

NURSE PITKIN: The sandman was his constant companion, as he slipped away in the arms of pneumonia, the old man's friend.

MACKIE: "But you can't push the glass but so far. Push it, and it pushes back. Sure enough a young gob gatherer burned his lungs so bad, he died 'fore the week was out. Well it was the war, really, that killed him. But the men blamed the Demerys anyways. They called strike."

PETER/MACKIE: "An' for the first time ever, all the Demery fires went out."

JACKIE: *(Throws a broken piece of glass back into the pile, disgusted.)* This is nuts. There isn't a single perfect piece left. You want to go on hunting, go on, but I'm through.

NURSE PITKIN: *(Remaining on the tray is single, poison blue pitkin. She goes to* PETER.*)* It's at a moment like this that a trained Story Nurse is invaluable to the flow of the narrative.

PETER: *(Takes the pitkin off the tray.)* "But when the men finally returned to work, and started loading the wood into the great center furnace, someone cried out, and pointed, and they all saw the ghost of the gob gatherer, floating there. The master blower picked up a poison blue pitkin and flung it at the ghost, as hard as he could."

JACKIE: *(She turns back to face* PETER. *She sees the flask.)* You found one!

PETER: "And the ghost caught it. He held it, turned it over in his hands, and saw that it was good. Looked at the Demery touch mark on the bottom, and nodded his head, yes. And in one giant burst of light and thunder, the fire in Archimedes roared to life."

JACKIE: That was perfect.

PETER: *(Holding the flask up so it catches the light)* Yes. It is.

JACKIE: No, I mean the story. You told it just the way Mackie did when we were little.

NURSE PITKIN: Perfect? Can something that is ninety-five percent flimflam, and only five percent truth be perfect?

VICTOR: You're wearing a blue hat. A blue hat…with feathers…

NURSE PITKIN: *(Referring to* ELIZABETH *and* VICTOR, *taking a step towards them.)* Sometimes.

ELIZABETH: My Lilli Ann hat had feathers! My Lilli Ann—the one I was wearing the day I met you!

VICTOR: Sky blue—with deep peach blow feathers.

ELIZABETH: *(She thrusts her knitting into the bag, determined to get up this time.)* I really think I'd better have a little talk with that anesthesiologist. That hat was a perfect shade of forest green.

VICTOR: No. I like it blue.

ELIZABETH: But it won't match my dress, my dress is a gray green crepe with—

VICTOR: You're not wearing that dress.

ELIZABETH: I'm not?

VICTOR: No.

ELIZABETH: Well, then I must be wearing my Mountain Home suit—the summer weight wool with the pink piping—

VICTOR: You're not wearing the Mountain Home either, Lizbeth.

ELIZABETH: I'm not.

VICTOR: No.

ELIZABETH: Well, I can't think what else I'd be wearing with that hat, I—

VICTOR: You're not wearing anything at all.

ELIZABETH: I'm meeting you for the first time stark buck naked?

VICTOR: Except for the hat.

ELIZABETH: Oh. *(Bravely)* What are you wearing, dear?

VICTOR: I'm wearing...I'm wearing... *(Struggles up from some soft deep place to find the answer.)* I'm wearing... you. *(His face shines with the joy of it. He takes her hand, and begins to sway and rock in a sweet, gentle rhythm.)*

ELIZABETH: The first time we met? *(Horrified. Agitated, she pulls her hand away from* VICTOR.*)* No, Victor—stop. It just isn't right.

VICTOR: I knew the minute I met you—

ELIZABETH: What will people think, Victor—

VICTOR: What people, Lizbeth? There's just you. And me. In the whole world, there's only you and me now. I knew the instant I saw you I was going to marry you, so who's to think? There's only you and me.

ELIZABETH: I knew it too, Victor, but—

VICTOR: Please?

ELIZABETH: Not on our first date, Victor, I just can't.

(VICTOR's face falls into sadness.)

ELIZABETH: But I could… (She shyly plays with a flower growing in her lap.) I could think about our wedding night… (She timidly reaches out, and touches his hand. She closes her eyes, and begins to sway with him, slowly.)

VICTOR: But the hat—

ELIZABETH: (Stops swaying, opens her eyes.) What?

VICTOR: Just this once—could you…?

(NURSE PITKIN hands VICTOR the hat. It is sky blue with peach blow feathers. He hands it to ELIZABETH.)

ELIZABETH: (She puts it on. She closes her eyes again, smiling.) Just this once.

(They sway together, softly.)

PETER: (Turning the flask over in his hands, inspecting it) Don't you think it's kind of spooky, a cobalt pitkin, turning up like this?

JACKIE: Oh, please—we a ran a batch of cobalt last month, used a lot of the old mold-blown styles, cobalt's always been popular so we do a lot of—

PETER: You ever batch any cobalt that looked like that, Jackie? And look at the lip—there's a mark, a signature, under the lip.

(She holds it up, tries to make it out.)

NURSE PITKIN: The Greeks called glass poured stone, and their slaves labored for weeks at a time, carving vessels out of solid blocks of it. Glass blowing began sometime in the first century, and the technique of mold-blowing was developed almost simultaneously. All early mold-blown glass was signed—sometimes by the glass blower, but always by the die-sinker, or mold maker. The earliest surviving pieces from Rome all carry the legend "Ennion made me." Other pieces with his mark carry this added inscription: "Let the buyer remember me."

JACKIE: It's not a signature, Peter—it's a scratch or crack we didn't get polished out or patched in the mold, that's all it is. It is not a sign from the sandman.

PETER: He's not going to like us doing this, Jackie.

JACKIE: I told you, Peter, Dad is—

PETER: Not Dad. The sandman.

JACKIE: You always were a sucker for that story.

PETER: Look, Jackie, there are tax shelters, loopholes, ways we can find to keep it going, if we—

JACKIE: There is no we, Peter. There's Dad and me, but there's no you and me. You're here today but tomorrow you'll be gone. Gone, back to your cozy, predictable, boring—

PETER: I can't believe you're starting in on this again! I can't believe you think you can make me feel guilty because I have a wife, and a job, and a life!

JACKIE: Well I can't believe you think this— *(Holding the blue pitkin in the air, shaking it.)* —is a sign from the sandman! But you know what—I wouldn't mind a sign myself. So I'll make you another deal, bucko.

(JACKIE throws the pitkin back to PETER.)

JACKIE: If the sandman catches it—if he looks at the Demery touch mark on the bottom, and nods his head yes—I won't call the bank. I won't make the call that erases the name Demery from the Demery Glassworks.

(JACKIE *and* PETER *head for the furnace/operating table.*)

(ELIZABETH *and* VICTOR *are still making love for the first time, in her memories, and in his dreams:*)

VICTOR: This is what it means to be safe.

ELIZABETH: This is what it means to be safe.

VICTOR: This is what it means to be somewhere with someone no one else can go.

ELIZABETH: You. You.

VICTOR: No place but you.

ELIZABETH: No place but you. I want ten children.

VICTOR: No place but— *(He opens his eyes.)* Ten children, Lizbeth?

ELIZABETH: Ten. Boy girl, boy girl, boy girl, girl girl, boy girl. Six girls.
Four boys. Girls are easier than boys. Ten. The boys will look like you.
The girls will look like me.

VICTOR: I don't think it works like that, Lizbeth. The boys will look like your mother, and the girls…the girls will….

ELIZABETH: I don't want my girls to look like your father, Victor.

NURSE PITKIN: *(She stands in front of the furnace, between it and* JACKIE *and* PETER.*)* It would be so easy. So easy. Just to reach out my hand, and catch the glass.

ELIZABETH: I'm frightened of your father.

PETER: Jackie?

JACKIE: Ready anytime you are.

NURSE PITKIN: It would make such a good story. I could just reach out my hand, and catch it. It would make this a perfect, old fashioned story. I sometimes yearn for the old story—it's an occupational hazard, in my line of work.

JACKIE: Ready?

PETER: Almost.

NURSE PITKIN: After all, the old stories had something in them that kept them from truly ending. Even if all the people in them died the story still went on. Something—the courage, or truth of those old stories endured.

PETER: Okay. Ready.

NURSE PITKIN: It would be such a small thing, to step into the role of the sandman, and catch the glass. It would make this whole story accelerate to the velocity of the great wheel, and conquer time. *(Reaches out her hands)* And Peter would never tire of telling his children about how the sandman caught the pitkin, and the Demery Glassworks was saved. And his children would tell their children. And their grandchildren would tell theirs. And—

PETER: ONE FOR THE SANDMAN! *(He "throws" the pitkin by pretending to throw it.)*

NURSE PITKIN: *(Holds up her hand, as if she is catching the pitkin—she is holding an exact duplicate of the pitkin, giving the illusion of catching it.)* But every responsible Story Nurse will tell you. The real story is that the story ends. For the hero. For the extras. For the story tellers. For the people to whom the story is told.

*(*NURSE PITKIN *lets the pitkin fall to the floor. It shatters.* PETER *walks up to the furnace, and begins picking up the broken pieces of the flask and putting them in his pocket.)*

JACKIE: You know, for a second there I thought he caught it. I really—

PETER: Forget it, Jackie.

JACKIE: But I did.

PETER: You never believed it, Jackie. You don't believe in anything you can't hold in your hands.

ELIZABETH: Victor, look at the babies. Look at how perfect they are.

VICTOR: *(Surprised and thrilled)* Lizbeth! One girl! One boy! Just like you said.

NURSE PITKIN: Peter Demery will be the first Demery in seven generations not to die of Demery Glass Heart or Demery Glass Lung, or a combination of both. He has his wife Penny to thank for that. His wife Penny, and his head for numbers, numbers which never left his hands free, and open to receive the glass.

VICTOR: Nine months to the day we were married. But who was counting?

ELIZABETH: Just the entire population of Crystal City, that's all.

VICTOR: You can see the day we made them—you can see—there! Our wedding night! There! In Jacqueline's shining eyes and melon hair. There! In Peter's little milk glass hands.

NURSE PITKIN: Numbers fit the hands exactly. Five is the largest number we can grasp with one hand, so our money comes to us in multiples of five. It turns out that numbers, like most man made things, retain the imprint of the hands that made them.

(Watching PETER *putting the glass in his pocket:)*

JACKIE: You know, it's funny—I guess I was so used to you doing that that I never really noticed you doing it.

But now that I am noticing, I have to say it. That is the stupidest thing I ever saw in my life.

NURSE PITKIN: He thinks he's escaped.

JACKIE: I mean, it's only a matter of time, right? Just a matter of time before you forget, and stick your hand in there, and—

PETER: I never forget.

NURSE PITKIN: He thinks he's escaped being broken by the story of Demery glass. Escaped the hated glass that slipped though his hands, that were full of numbers, escaped the scorching heat that blistered his face, escaped the aching thirst, the constant, aching thirst, that no amount of beer could ever slack.

ELIZABETH: I can still remember your father, marching into Saint Mary's like he owned it. I don't even think he heard the nurses screaming at him, he just barreled into the nursery, scooped up Jackie and Peter, held them up in the air, one in each big hand.

VICTOR: (Holding his hands up in the air, as if full of something) "Two Demerys at one blow" he said. "That's economy. That's efficiency."

NURSE PITKIN: He is young, and smart, and his children are sound, and healthy. He thinks he has slipped out of the grasp of this story, into a new one.

JACKIE: I wish you'd stop doing that, Peter.

PETER: I'll put it in my goddamn pocket if I goddamn want to.

NURSE PITKIN: He thinks he has slipped into a better story. One with a happy ending. One with an ending unlike the one his family has lived its life telling.

VICTOR: "A pair of drinking glasses" he said. "A matched set."

NURSE PITKIN: He has only escaped into the same story, with different details, but there's no telling him that now. He doesn't know yet that whether you make your life out of glass or numbers— *(She holds out her hands.)* —the story is the same.

VICTOR: *(He lowers his hands.)* I'm sorry, Lizbeth. I know you wanted eight more—ten children, boy, girl, boy, girl, girl, girl, boy—

ELIZABETH: There wasn't enough money for ten, I could see that.

VICTOR: But—

ELIZABETH: I'm not an idiot, Victor. You tried to hide what was happening at the works from me, but I could tell.

VICTOR: I'm sorry, I—

ELIZABETH: About what! About two perfect, healthy children? There's nothing to be sorry about.

JACKIE: You've got to stop doing that, Peter.

PETER: No I don't.

JACKIE: It's stupid.

PETER: Yeah. So?

JACKIE: So stop it.

(He doesn't.)

JACKIE: You're making me nervous, Peter, stop it. Peter—

(JACKIE grabs PETER's arm to get him to stop, he screams at her, wrenching his arm out of her grasp.)

PETER: Leave me the fuck alone Penny!

JACKIE/PENNY: (NURSE PITKIN, *transformed into* PENNY *again, appears from behind the furnace.)* I hate it when you call me/her Penny!

PETER: Shit. Not again.

JACKIE/PENNY: What's wrong—did you cut yourself?

PETER: No.

JACKIE/PENNY: You sure?

PETER: I DID NOT CUT MYSELF!

JACKIE: It's inevitable, Peter. People who play with fire get burned.

JACKIE/PENNY: And people who play with glass get—

PETER: NO!

VICTOR: Smaller. Smaller. Specialize. That's the ticket now, you want to stay alive in business. Or bigger… bigger—dominate—monopolize—but bigger was out of the question, with Peter gone. If we had just been big enough to get bigger or small enough to get smaller…we were always the wrong size.

ELIZABETH: No. The exact right size. For booths, in restaurants, for driving, in the car, for sitting at the kitchen table. For everything. A perfect size for a family. The two of us, the two of them. The perfect size.

VICTOR: I tried so hard. I tried so hard—and we almost made it, Lizbeth. Almost. And then all the strength fell out of my body with a loud crash.

JACKIE/PENNY: Empty your pocket!

PETER: No.

PENNY: Empty it, Peter. It's time to leave all that broken glass behind.

PETER: I can't—

JACKIE: You hate the glass, don't you?

PETER: What?

JACKIE: You hate it, you always have.

PETER: Hate it? You're crazy! You don't know anything about me!

JACKIE/PENNY: I know you better than anyone in the world.

PETER: Do you?

JACKIE: I know you did everything you could to get away from here. I know you married the last woman on earth who had any intention of letting you come back.

PETER: But do you know why? Tell me, Jackie, if you know me so well. Tell me why I left. Tell me why I ran and never once looked back. Tell me!

PENNY: She doesn't why. She doesn't know why, but I do. *(To* JACKIE*)* He saw the sandman.

JACKIE: No.

PENNY: Hurry, Peter, empty your pocket before it's too late.

JACKIE: You're lying! If you had seen him, you would have told me.

PETER: Why?

JACKIE: Because—we told each other everything.

PETER: So?

PENNY: Peter, you don't have to do this, you don't—

JACKIE: What are you talking about, do what, do—

PENNY: Peter— *(Pulls him toward her.)*

JACKIE: Peter— *(Pulls him toward her.)*

JACKIE/PENNY: *(They turn on each other.)* I HATE YOUR WIFE/SISTER. SHE WANTS YOU TO BE SOMETHING YOU'RE NOT SUPPOSED TO BE.

PETER: No. It's me. I'm the one who wants to be something I can't be.

VICTOR: I'm blowing a bubble. A glass bubble. So big. So light. I'm taking in the biggest breath. I'm blowing a bubble. So big. When it gets big enough, Elizabeth, we'll get in. The two of us together. And sail away.

ELIZABETH: Sail away. From all this.

VICTOR: It's so perfect, Lizbeth. So light. So fine. A bubble of breath and fire—it's cooling now, but can you see—can you see the fire in it, the halo fading from red to orange to gold to silver, before it disappears?

ELIZABETH: Yes, Victor. I can see.

VICTOR: Not long now. When the fire is out. When the color is gone.

PETER: The glass loved you, Jackie, it did anything you wanted, but me? I didn't have the hands. Every piece of glass I touched was flawed. One night I tried—I tried so hard. For hours, here alone, five then ten then fifteen vases, simple little vases—good enough for somebody who wasn't named Demery, but for a Demery—not good at all. I was down to the tail end of the batch, there was one gather left, I got it, worked it, prayed. I thought, yes. This one will be perfect. It started to cool. And when I saw how flawed a thing it was—I got so angry I threw it against Archimedes, as hard as I could.

VICTOR: Almost ready now. Almost.

PETER: But it didn't break. The sandman was standing there. He caught it. He held it up, looked at it. And he said—

PETER/VICTOR: I know you're afraid.

ELIZABETH: Not as long as you're here.

PETER: I know the glass slips through your fingers.

PETER/VICTOR: I know you don't know what to do.

VICTOR: But trust me a little while longer, Lizbeth. It's strong enough. To carry us both. To carry us through.

PETER: And then he let it fall—he let it fall, and it shattered on the floor.

VICTOR: It's ready, Lizbeth. Don't be afraid.

PETER: The pieces were like stars in the furnace light—stars scattered on the ground. I wanted to stand there and look at them forever. But then he picked them up. He held them tight, in his hand. I could see them begin to glow—to go through all the colors backwards—from clear to gold to molten orange.
And then he opened his hand.

(The waiting-room couch and the chair begin to elevate, and fly, taking ELIZABETH *and* VICTOR *very close to the audience.)*

ELIZABETH: Oh, Victor. It's so lovely, like this. Sailing away. Sailing somewhere no one else can go.

PETER: And it was the most beautiful thing I've ever seen. Part flower, part liquid, part ice. And all of it was made out of moving, burning water.

ELIZABETH: So high. So high now. Up over the tree tops. So fast, so far. The lakes are plates of glass, they're mirrors spilled on the landscape—look, the sun's setting—Victor, the sunset turns the rivers and the streams into stained glass windows, flowing along the ground.

PETER: And he said—when you can do this, Peter. When you are not afraid to do this. Then you will know. Who you are supposed to be. *(He puts his hand in his pocket.)* SHIT.

JACKIE: *(Grabbing his hand, too late)* No—

PETER: Penny!

JACKIE: Stop calling me Penny!

PETER: I am not calling you Penny, I am calling my wife. I am calling her name. Penny?

PENNY: I'm here.

PETER: *(He turns to* NURSE PITKIN/PENNY, *holds out his bleeding hand.)* See? I did it.

PENNY: I see. *(She touches his hand, gently.)* I've been waiting seven years for you to do that, Peter. From the first night we met, I've been waiting for you to forget and put your hand in your pocket. Your pocket, which was always full of broken glass.
I'm glad I don't have to wait any longer. *(She takes off the paper doll cutout costume. Underneath there is a simple white version of* PENNY *in an everyday skirt and shirt.)*
Call as soon as there's news about your father. The girls miss you already. *(She turns back, and kisses him.)*
I miss you too. *(She "leaves" and immediately begins her transformation, probably behind the furnace again, into* NURSE PITKIN.*)*

ELIZABETH: Oh, Victor. It's so lovely, so—WAIT! VICTOR—GO BACK—we've forgotten the children— there's no room for them—

VICTOR: They're already gone, sweetheart—

ELIZABETH: No—they're here with us—here—there are four of us—I buy everything in fours, four lamb chops, four ears of corn, four Danish for Sunday breakfast— surely there's room for four here—not for a big family with eight or ten children, maybe—but for a family of four, Victor—

VICTOR: Gone. Peter, already. And we have to let Jackie go too.

ELIZABETH: Go back for them, Victor. Now.

VICTOR: Too late, sweetheart.

ELIZABETH: No. NO! We made a good life—we made it good and strong! What's wrong with our lives? Is there something wrong with the life we made, did we do something wrong?

VICTOR: Lizbeth—remember what you said last night—

ELIZABETH: I didn't mean this—I only wanted you to be safe—I only wanted—

VICTOR: It's gone, Elizabeth. You made me promise. And I promised.

ELIZABETH: No, I won't let you—why should the bank get it? It means nothing to them. Real estate, that's all it is.

VICTOR: I told Jackie to go ahead and call Mister Connally at the bank.

ELIZABETH: But why? We've got to keep it for Jackie—

VICTOR: Let her go, Lizbeth. Before it's too late for her. Let her go. Let her start by calling the bank.

ELIZABETH: (*She looks around wildly, calling for her.*) But they'll sell it to developers, they'll turn it into a condo or a restaurant or one of those damn boutique malls. JACKIE! Don't do it, Jackie—come back, Jackie—

VICTOR: Shhh, Lizbeth. The glass is gone.

NURSE PITKIN: There is never a moment when we believe nothing.

PETER: (*Gasping with pain, he pulls his hand out of his pocket, clenched in a tight fist, full of glass. Blood begins to appear.*) Didn't you—didn't you always wonder what it would feel like?

JACKIE: I know what it feels like. It hurts.

VICTOR: Maybe we'll move up to Saint Louis. Be closer to Peter's kids that way, watch 'em growing up.

PETER: You grow up in a world of glass, and every piece of it an invitation.

JACKIE: Even if you haven't severed the tendons you could still lose your hand! Peter, don't you remember about infection from the dust—don't you remember what happens when you get cut here?

NURSE PITKIN: There is never a moment when we do not believe that we believe the right something.

PETER: Nobody ever gets cut here.

ELIZABETH: It can't be over—it just started—

VICTOR: It's not over, sweetheart. It's just different now.

(The couch and chair stop their flight, and begin slowly to return to the stage.)

JACKIE: Look at my hands, Peter. Look! They look like Granddad's and Dad's and Mackie's hands. Nobody ever gets cut here…. Didn't you ever notice a single thing that happened here?

PETER: I noticed. I noticed the glass.

NURSE PITKIN: The struggle to believe in the right something—in the something that will save us—is always a compelling story—regardless of the telling details.

PETER: I noticed every time it didn't break.

(Lights surround the operating table, where DR GLASS and his TEAM are in motion.)

DR GLASS: All right. Keep your eye on the clock, Stu, this is for the money, boys. Here we go, smooth and regular, everybody stay in sequence, tag and seal.

(The couch and chair lurch, VICTOR gasps in pain.)

VICTOR: Something's—something's—something's happening, Elizabeth. I don't—I can't—we almost made it, Lizbeth. I almost— *(He begins to breathe with difficulty, as he begins to become disoriented, and the couch, in jerky, frightening movements, returns to the waiting room.)* —we finally got small enough, Lizbeth, and then the pain—the pain—bigger than the whole world—

ELIZABETH: VICTOR!!!!!

(The couch and the chair crash the last few inches, onto the stage. VICTOR falls from his seat, onto his knees, in pain.)

ELIZABETH: VICTOR! Don't leave me—you promised you wouldn't leave me—VICTOR!!! Remember what you promised me!

VICTOR: The pain…so big…bigger than the whole world…

(NURSE PITKIN assists him as he slowly moves away from ELIZABETH, toward the operating theater.)

ELIZABETH: Damn it. Damn it. Just like an idiot, I've used up the past, I've used it up, and he's still in there, and there's nothing left of my life but this nightmare. There's nothing left of my life but this.

(NURSE PITKIN helps VICTOR lie down on the operating table.)

DR GLASS: Get him stabilized, watch the core temperature, coooool it down, slow, slow, slower— watch it now—

ELIZABETH: What would an idiot wish for now. What! …I KNOW WHAT AN IDIOT WOULD WISH FOR IN A HOSPITAL WAITING ROOM AT A MOMENT LIKE THIS! A CIGARETTE!

(NURSE PITKIN produces a cigarette, gives it to ELIZABETH, lights it for her. She smokes. She stabs out the cigarette in an ashtray NURSE PITKIN holds.)

ELIZABETH: No—this isn't the cigarette I want. This isn't the cigarette I need. I need a very specific cigarette. I need...I need....

DR GLASS: More light—yeah, over there. Here we go.

ELIZABETH: I want...I want...I want a Herbert Taryton. No filter, smooth cut—a rich blend of fine tobaccos in the white and blue pack—and I don't want just any Herbert Taryton—I WANT THE LAST HERBERT TARYTON I EVER SMOKED ON JUNE 18TH, 1965— MY THIRTIETH BIRTHDAY!

(NURSE PITKIN *produces a pack of Herbert Tarytons—with one cigarette in it.* ELIZABETH *takes it, lights it herself. Smokes it with great passion.*)

CANDY STRIPER: (*Enters tap dancing. She is a dazzling cute candy striper, in white and pink uniform, fresh as the morning dew, carrying a fire extinguisher.*)
You can't smoke (*Tap-tap tap*)
(*She extinguishes* ELIZABETH's *cigarette with a little blast of the extinguisher.*)
You can't smoke (*Tap-tap tap*)
It's no joke (*Tap-tap tap*)
It's a no smoking zoooooooonnnnnnnneee!
(*A tapping flourish*)

ELIZABETH: You've—ruined it...RUINED IT! YOU'VE RUINED MY LAST CIGARETTE!

CANDY STRIPER: (*Doing tap-turns with each phrase.*)
Now don't moan and don't groan
All the studies have shown
That you shouldn't postpone it
And we can't condone it
Though half of our business
Is known to come from it

ELIZABETH: How DARE you tell me I can't smoke—
how DARE you tell me I can't do the only goddamn
fucking thing I want to do that I can!

CANDY STRIPER: YOU—CAN'T SMOKE YOU CAN'T
SMOKE YOU CAN'T SMOKE YOU CAN'T SMOKE
*(She continues singing, whirling, tapping, a dervish in pink
and white.)*

NURSE PITKIN: *(Hands* ELIZABETH *a gun)* Sometimes—
it's just the little things that help. The little assistance
here, the helping hand there. I remember, just last
week we had a double O double T—Out Of Town
Terminal—whose family needed some help making
the shipping arrangements for the body. Well, I sat
right down at my station and made a few simple calls.
It really wasn't much. But it meant so much to that
family.

CANDY STRIPER: YOU CAN'T SMOKE YOU CAN'T
SMOKE YOU CAN'T SMOKE YOU CAN'T

*(*ELIZABETH *shoots* CANDY STRIPER. *She falls dead on the
floor, dropping the fire extinguisher.)*

NURSE PITKIN: *(As she drags the* CANDY STRIPER *off stage.)*
You have no idea how many candy stripers we lose
this way.

ELIZABETH: Oh, dear. I didn't mean to do that—well,
I mean, I did mean to do it, I just didn't mean for it
to really—I mean…killing me or making me strong,
killing me or making me strong, killing me or making
me strong…well, it's made me strong enough to kill.
Either I don't know how to be an idiot—or I'm doing
a little too well. *(She picks up her knitting, starts knitting
again.)*

STELLA: *(Enters, without* JOSEPHINE, *sees* ELIZABETH
sitting there, sits next to her. She takes a scarf out of her

huge pocketbook, and begins knitting. The two women knit together for a moment.) Hello.

ELIZABETH: Hello.

STELLA: Here with your husband?

ELIZABETH: Yes.

STELLA: I'm here with mine. Three hours he's in there. Yours?

ELIZABETH: Five hours.

STELLA: *(Knowingly, nods her head)* Five hours. *(Indicating the sweater* ELIZABETH *is knitting)* For yourself?

ELIZABETH: No. *(She holds it up off her lap so* STELLA *can see it—it is enormous.)* For my daughter.

STELLA: Hmm. Big girl.

ELIZABETH: *(She suddenly notices that it is quite large.)* Oh. *(She crumples it up in her lap, but keeps knitting.)* Well. I guess I sort of got carried away.

STELLA: Take it from me—I know. *(She starts pulling the scarf out of her purse.)* Stay away from sweaters when you're here. Scarves. Afghans. Shawls. *(The scarf is infinitely long.)* They're safe. An extra foot or two, who can tell? Who's to know? Take it from me, I know.

*(*ELIZABETH *and* STELLA *knit together, silently, for a moment.)*

STELLA: When my husband sleeps his chest fills up with birds. Sparrows and hummingbirds and sea gulls that are far away. Tiny birds, specks on the horizon. Bits of movement, fragments of sound that come in pieces through the wet sea air.
His lungs are turning into ocean. Soft and saline. His chest grows bigger and bigger—a barrel chest, the doctors call it. Emphysema chest. The lung cavity,

bellowing out. The doctors say it is a symptom. But my husband knows. And I know.

His chest is growing bigger and bigger, to save the birds. To give them air, and room to fly and live. But it can't grow fast enough. The tiny birds are multiplying. There are thousands of them, and there's no room. The tiny birds are drowning.

We hear them as the slow tide inside my husband rises, thousands of them beating their wings and crying from far away. Drowning in the soft ocean. As the water reclaims the land. Inside my husband.

At night I lie in bed beside him. And I listen to them sing.

(STELLA *gets up.* ELIZABETH *tries to comfort her, but the vines and flowers restrain her.* STELLA *slowly walks off stage.* ELIZABETH *becomes more and more agitated, trying to set herself free.*)

ELIZABETH: Could—could somebody please help me? Jackie? Peter! JACKIE. JACKIE!!!!

JACKIE: Does it hurt much, Peter?

PETER: What do you think?

JACKIE: I think it feels like you're holding a handful of fire.

(DR GLASS *and the* TEAM *have evolved past glass makers, and will have shamanisitic and voodoo elements worked into their costumes during the following sequence. There is something of the earth, and old ceremonies, in the procedures they now perform.*)

DR GLASS: Watch the flow—keep it steady—

ELIZABETH: SOMEBODY HELP ME PLEASE!!!

JACKIE: It's time. (*She gets up, to go.*) I'm going to call the bank.

PETER: Jackie, wait—

JACKIE: No. He made me promise that when he came out from under the anesthesia, it'd be gone.

JOE:I don't like the color—

DR GLASS: Give me some room—

PETER: You're lying. He wouldn't do that. He would have talked to me first.

JACKIE: Why? You left, Peter.

DR GLASS: Come on, come on, let me see some color here.

PETER: He still would have asked me. The glass is yours, but the works are mine!

JACKIE: Then why did you go away! Why didn't you stay!

PETER: I couldn't!

JACKIE: Mom and Dad needed you! I needed you.

ELIZABETH: *(Exhausted from thrashing and ripping at the vines)* SOMEBODY HELP ME GET FREE OF THIS! SOMEBODY PLEASE HELP ME GET FREE!

JACKIE: He wouldn't be sick, everything would be like it used to be, if you had just stayed!

PETER: You stayed and it didn't help, did it!

ELIZABETH: HELP ME WAKE UP FROM THIS NIGHTMARE, HELP ME GET UP AND RUN OUT THE DOOR! SOMEBODY HELP ME GET FREE!

JOE: Color still poor.

PETER: You stayed, you threw your life away—

JACKIE: Oh, you have got your nerve—

PETER: It's the truth, Jackie! Stuck here, no life at all but mom and dad and the works—

JACKIE: At least I tried—

PETER: So what! So you loved the glass! You still couldn't save it. What chance did I have!

JACKIE: It wasn't the glass, Peter. The glass stayed the same. It was the numbers—everything about the numbers changed! You love numbers, that's what we needed. We needed you. If you had stayed—

PETER: That's not fair.

JACKIE: We'd still have the works. And Dad would be fine. And—

PETER: Stop saying that! You know that's not true!

JOE: It's fading. Color is fading.

JACKIE: I don't care. I wish it were true. I wish everything could have a different ending, where things could just go on the way they used to be,<R>

and nothing bad would ever happen to us.

ELIZABETH: I DON'T KNOW HOW TO DO THIS!!

JOE: Gray. Color is gray.

ELIZABETH: I DON'T KNOW HOW AND I DON'T WANT TO KNOW HOW!

JACKIE: That's what I wish, and I don't care how unfair it is to you.

NURSE PITKIN: There is always a belief that there is a way, or a word, that will work magic.

PETER: *(Holding her)* Oh, Jackie. Everybody wishes that! But nobody gets that particular wish to come true.

(DR GLASS *and the* TEAM *have woodland aspects to their costumes, and there may be something like spinning, in the procedure they now perform.)*

DR GLASS: *(Working furiously)* Is it gold yet?

JOE: Color is fading.

DR GLASS: IS IT GOLD YET?

CLINT: No.

NURSE PITKIN: There is always the belief that there is a word that can be cried out, let loose in the world—that there is a power—unleashed in syllables—corseted in consonants—knee-deep in vowels, running over, brimming over, in a rush of sounds. A word that rides on the human voice, to work its magic in the world.

DR GLASS: *(Screaming)* IS IT—

JOE: No! We're losing him—

NURSE PITKIN: *(Steely pronouncement, slow, precise)* Rumplestiltskin.

JOE: Wait!

NURSE PITKIN: Rumplestiltskin! The magic name. Invoked! Proclaimed! The magic name that, at this point in all true narratives, is used the way great magic names in narratives are always used. In vain. By small mortal things. In mortal pain.

JOE: We're losing him—he's slipping away, I can't—

CLINT: He's coding! He's coding!

NURSE PITKIN: *(Calling it out, loudly and clearly, and big)* RUMPLESTILTSKIN! Say it with all your might. There are no magic words at this moment in the story. All the magic in words has run out.

(Blackout everywhere except the operating theater, where there is only the body of the patient on the table, and the TEAM *of surgeons, disguised only as surgeons, working feverishly to save him, in blinding white light, and small spots on* ELIZABETH, *knitting, and* JACKIE *and* PETER.*)*

DR GLASS: GET ON GET ON GET ON—Now.

*(*ELIZABETH *is knitting furiously.)*

CLINT: Nothing. I'M GETTING NOTHING!!!

(Sound effects of an actual operating theater begin to be audible—the beeping of the heart monitor, the whoosh of the heart-lung machine, etc.)

DR GLASS: Joe—massage—match me—one, two, one, two—

JOE/DR GLASS : One, two, one, two—

(JOE takes over the massage.)

ELIZABETH: I can't…I just can't…figure out a way….

DR GLASS: Let's get back on—

JOE: Up the dopamine—

CLINT: Color is poor—

STU: Pressure is down.

ELIZABETH: *(Her knitting spills from her lap.)* Help me God, please somebody help me. I don't know how to do this. I've tried every way I know and I can't figure it out. I don't know how to sit out here, I don't know how to do this. I can't do this. Please.

STU: Pressure is down.

NURSE PITKIN: The problem with good stories is that they are nothing like life. Good stories tie things up, make them smooth and continuous. Stories are not things that break. In stories, moments of greatness arrive, and—

STU: Pressure is down.

CLINT: Oxygen saturation still low.

DR GLASS: Speed up the machine, rev it up REV IT UP—

JOE: More K—give him more K—

CLINT: Not looking good. Color is poor.

NURSE PITKIN: In stories the chance for greatness always arrives—and stays.

DR GLASS: Heads up—coming off the machine again—

NURSE PITKIN: Even in tragedy, where the moment of greatness is lost, where the point of the story IS that greatness slips through our hands, the story itself grabs up greatness in its greedy little fingers.

STU: Pressure is down.

DR GLASS: Get him back on—

CLINT: Color is poor—

NURSE PITKIN: The story scoops up greatness in a handful of words, and rewrites the pain of living into something good and grand. This transformation is accomplished by the story's perfection.
That is a great story's tragedy. It is perfect.

DR GLASS: Let's try it again—coming off—now—

STU: Holding his own.

DR GLASS: Come on, come on—

NURSE PITKIN: The purpose of great stories is to tell a lie about life. The lie that pain is good. That dreams come true. That heroes act heroically.

STU: Holding. Holding.

JOE: Looking good.

PETER: I think it's happening, Jackie. Just like the sandman promised.

NURSE PITKIN: Story. S-T-O-R-Y.
Sty sot sort
toy toys
troy try
rot rots—
(Pause)
rosy

PETER: *(Holding out his bleeding hand, in front of him)* It's going to be wonderful, Jackie.

STU: Holding his own.

NURSE PITKIN: There is nothing true or human in perfection—

DR GLASS: Get his pulse up, Joe.

NURSE PITKIN: —except the struggle toward it.

JOE: Looking good.

DR GLASS: Looks like he's out of the woods.

NURSE PITKIN: We are stuck with stories that lie, and do not break.

DR GLASS: Let's close him up.

(Lights begin to fade on the operating theater.)

NURSE PITKIN: We are stuck with lives that break. But are true.

(NURSE PITKIN hands JACKIE a phone.)

JACKIE: Mister Connally? It's Jackie Demery. Yes. He came through it fine. He'll sign the papers tomorrow. Yes. Thank you. We do too. *(She puts the phone down on the master's chair. The chair bursts into flames.)* It's gone.

PETER: Look Jackie. *(He starts to open his hand. There is a glow, a light coming from inside his fist.)*

NURSE PITKIN: Yes, look—everybody look—there it is— the thing Jackie and Peter Demery have lived all their lives for—there it is—shining in his hands.

PETER: It's happening just like he said—

(JACKIE puts her hands around PETER's fist, the glow emanates from both their hands.)

NURSE PITKIN: Yes—just like the sandman said. If the hero can stand the pain—if the heroine can stand the fire—they will end up with something beautiful made out of the work and faith and pain, they will hold something perfect in their hands. They will end up triumphant as the tale comes to its end. *(She picks up the fire extinguisher the* CANDY STRIPER *dropped.)*

JACKIE: It's perfect.

NURSE PITKIN: *(As she approaches them, steadily, holding the extinguisher almost ceremonially.)* And now, you're about to see it.

PETER: Just like he promised.

NURSE PITKIN: Just like a good story promises. It's what you came here for, isn't it? Yes, of course it is. It's an old, old, story, the promise of work. A story spanning the ages, repeated and passed down through the generations, told by father to son, mother to daughter, the story of, the glory of work. And now, it is the end of that story. Naturally, you expect you're going to see its perfect end.

*(*NURSE PITKIN *extinguishes the burning chair just as* PETER *is about to open his hand.)*

(All stage lights fade as the fire dies, with the exception of a tiny spot on NURSE PITKIN and her extinguisher.

NURSE PITKIN: I hate stories. But I love story tellers.

*(*NURSE PITKIN'*s spot goes. Lights up on an area of bare stage, as in the Prologue.)*

(Three three-sided glass barriers, identical to the one constructed in the prologue, are flown in/brought on. But this time they are turned so that the open side is facing the audience. JACKIE *enters.)*

JACKIE: And this really did happen. Of all these true things, that did not happen, but are still true, this one really did. It is as true as I can make it, but you should know that glass forgery is the easiest forgery to make, and the hardest to see. Bear that in mind.

*(NURSE PITKIN and ELIZABETH enter, from opposite sides
of the stage. NURSE PITKIN is carrying three identical
bundles.)*

NURSE PITKIN: There is only one story. One true story.
It ends like this. All true stories arrive, at last, in the
body of the story teller, in the story the story teller
cannot escape.

*(NURSE PITKIN hands a bundle to ELIZABETH, and one to
JACKIE, keeping one for herself. Each woman goes to a glass
enclosure.)*

NURSE PITKIN: All true stories end like this.

*(The bundles contain an identical costume change. The
three women change into the woman JACKIE describes in
the following speech, removing their other costumes, which
they leave in a puddle at their feet. They have been wearing
simple full slips—a slip that the woman in the elevator
would wear—beneath their earlier costumes.)*

JACKIE: I was on my way up to my father's room in
the hospital, a few days after the operation. I was on
the elevator. The doors opened. A woman stepped
in. She was—I don't know. Sixty-five. Seventy. But
seventy the way seventy is in the farmland of our
fairy tale American myth. Her faded hair was braided,
and wrapped tightly at the back of her neck. Her face
was—careworn. Right out of the movies. Auntie Em
in the Wizard of Oz looked less like Auntie Em then
she did. She was wearing a cotton print dress, calico or
plaid, washed a thousand times. She was straight, and
tall, and there was a plain gold band on her left hand.
And she was fine, until she stepped onto the elevator.
But as soon as the doors slid shut she started to break.
And I was standing right there, I didn't know what
to do, if I touched her she'd shatter. She had used up
everything to make it into that elevator, she'd walked
those steps to the door at unimaginable cost, she had

lasted until the doors closed and what could I say to
her? What words would I use? What was the use of
any of the words I knew.

I started to reach out, but I couldn't touch her. I asked
her "Is there anything I can do, Ma'am?" She shook her
head. She sobbed, and the elevator climbed, forever,
the elevator climbed three floors, forever. At last the
doors slid open, and somehow I stepped out. And I
walked blindly—just like they do in novels—blindly
down the hall. I made it to my father's room, and I told
him about the woman in the elevator. About how she
had stood there, and just shattered.

And for the first time in my life, I saw my father cry.
And my question is, how is it that I was made, by the
best hands, out of love and care, to carry something
magnificent inside me—and I am not good enough.
To be what I was crafted to be. How is it that I have
dreamed all my life, of greatness, but I was only good
enough to carry that story to my father. Without the
courage or heart or knowledge to touch it. In a way
that could change the pain. *(She takes off the glass bead
necklace.)* And as I watched my father cry I knew the
truth. The inevitable, cold sad truth. I will not flow,
in the goodness of time. I will not melt, and make my
way to any universal, grace filled collective sea. I will
shatter, inevitably, into pieces, like all the rest before
me and behind me and in front of me.

*(All three women stand alone, inside their glass enclosure.
They are all the woman in the elevator.)*

NURSE PITKIN: The day I met him—all the pieces of the
world fell into place. I could almost feel the click.

ELIZABETH: Now I could stop struggling to make sense
out of things—oh, just because you grow up on a farm
doesn't mean you don't think, you know. Just because

you rise with the sun—and the barnyard animals are your friends—

JACKIE: —doesn't mean you don't think. So I did think. About a lot of things. And the minute I met him, I knew I could stop thinking about most of 'em.

ELIZABETH: You might think a person would be ashamed to say that, right out. But I'm not. I was happy and proud to have a man standing beside me who meant that I could stop thinking and worrying and get down to things.

NURSE PITKIN: To the real things.

ELIZABETH: Someone to work beside me.

JACKIE: Someone to pull together with and never worry about my back, never worry there was no one on my side.

NURSE PITKIN: A partner for the day and its work, and the night and its rest.

ELIZABETH: He was a good man. A good husband, good father. I could almost hear that little click nine, ten times a day.

JACKIE: I didn't have to think about things, or put them together—

NURSE PITKIN: They were already put.

JACKIE: They made sense.

ELIZABETH: I'm not saying that I ever fully understood about the night, though.

JACKIE: I didn't have to give the day and its work a second thought—

ELIZABETH: —but the night and its rest—

NURSE PITKIN: That click was different. I never really understood that portion of our lives, what happened at night, between us, I never understood.

JACKIE: I'd thought about it quite a lot before we'd gotten married, no different than any other seventeen-year-old girl—

ELIZABETH: —and I was relieved to be able to stop thinking about it, once I realized it was nothing you could really think about. But the night and its rest—

NURSE PITKIN: I never understood it the way I understood the day—except I knew that it was good.

ELIZABETH: People talk about it all the time, sex, sex, sex, but they never say "It's good—good the way work is, and bringing up three strong healthy children is, and having the respect of your neighbors, and standing for something is."

NURSE PITKIN: No one ever says that about it.

ELIZABETH: But it's true.

NURSE PITKIN: There's something I don't quite understand about it, but I know that's true.

ELIZABETH: I can still fit into my wedding dress. I know you hear a woman say that, you feel kind of sorry for them, you think, just another sad, old dried up woman with all the sweetness sweated out of her, bragging about fitting into an old yellowed dress no one alive even remembers her wearing.

JACKIE: But it's not bragging.

NURSE PITKIN: Not vanity either, or pride.

ELIZABETH: It's just this little voice inside you saying "I'm still the same person I was that day."

NURSE PITKIN: "I'm still standing in front of the preacher with my whole life ahead of me. I'm young and strong and I'm ready to pay."

JACKIE: "I am ready for the work, and I will pay."

ELIZABETH: So. I can still fit into my wedding dress.

NURSE PITKIN: I can still feel what I felt that day.

ELIZABETH: Let me go back and stand there again, I'll say it again. I'll still say I'll pay.

JACKIE: I'll work hard, with this man beside me, and between us, we'll pay.

ELIZABETH: And I knew, in the back of my mind, that this day—today—would come—that this day was part of it—

NURSE PITKIN: What I had to pay—

JACKIE: Part of the price you have to pay for standing there beside him.

ELIZABETH: I'm not saying I didn't know that the day would come when he wouldn't be there, beside me—I understood that the day would come, and I would stand here, alone—but I didn't realize, somehow, that he wouldn't be there during the night.

NURSE PITKIN: As if I understood part of what death is, but had completely left the other part out.

ELIZABETH: The day and its work, the night and its rest.

JACKIE: There they are, right together, you don't get one without the other.

ELIZABETH: They talk about it all the time, but they never really tell you. They tell you all kind of stories, but the stories never tell you so you know.

NURSE PITKIN: They tell you all kind of stories—

JACKIE: But the stories never tell you so you know.

ELIZABETH: I just didn't know about the night. That's all I'm saying.

NURSE PITKIN: And not a single story tells you so you know.

JACKIE: That's all I'm saying.

ELIZABETH: That's all I'm saying.

NURSE PITKIN: That's all I'm saying.

(Blackout)

END OF PLAY